L. M. Alcott

SIGNATURE OF REFORM

L. M. Alcott

SIGNATURE OF REFORM

EDITED BY

MADELEINE B. STERN

NORTHEASTERN UNIVERSITY PRESS
BOSTON

Northeastern University Press

Copyright 2002 by Madeleine B. Stern

Library of Congress Cataloging-in-Publication Data

L. M. Alcott : signature of reform / edited by Madeleine B. Stern.

p.   cm.

Includes index.

ISBN 1-55553-513-5 (acid-free paper)—

ISBN 1-55553-512-7 (pbk. : acid-free paper)

1. Alcott, Louisa May, 1832–1888—Political and social views—Sources.   2. Literature and society—United States—History—19th century—Sources.   3. Social problems in literature—Sources.   I. Stern, Madeleine B., 1912– II. Alcott, Louisa May, 1832–1888. Selections. 2002.

PS1018 .L3   2002

813'.4—dc21   2001059187

Designed by Joyce C. Weston

Composed in Minion by Coghill Composition, Richmond, Virginia. Printed and bound by Edwards Brothers, Inc., Lillington, North Carolina. The paper is EB Natural, an acid-free stock.

MANUFACTURED IN THE UNITED STATES OF AMERICA

06   05   04   03   02   5   4   3   2   1

Contents

Acknowledgments

I owe the title of this book to my lifelong friend and partner, Dr. Leona Rostenberg. I owe the concept and much of the contents of this book to the individuals listed at the end of my Introduction, especially to Jan Turnquist, director of the Orchard House, Concord, Massachusetts, and Professor Sarah Elbert of the State University of New York at Binghamton. To Jan Turnquist I am also grateful for her reading and critical evaluation of the typescript.

In addition, I am indebted to the following for supplying certain selections: Scott Duvall of the Harold B. Lee Library, Brigham Young University, Provo, Utah; George Fletcher, Director, and Wayne Furman and Elie Weitsman of New York Public Library's Special Collections; Katharine Houghton of New York; Dr. Norman Kanof of New York; Jan Turnquist of Concord, Massachusetts; and Barbara Williams, Archivist, Archives and Special Collections, MCP Hahnemann University, Philadelphia, Pennsylvania.

I am especially grateful to my editor at Northeastern University Press, John Weingartner, for his understanding and supportiveness, and to my copyeditor, Ann Twombly, for her scrupulous care and precision.

Introduction

The nineteenth century teemed with wrongs that induced Americans, especially New Englanders, to champion their reform. Of all those New Englanders—the abolitionists who agitated against slavery, the egalitarians who challenged antifeminism—the writer who consistently touched the nation's heartstrings and tempered its spirit, addressing herself often to the young, but reaching older generations, was the spinster Scheherazade from Concord, Massachusetts, Louisa May Alcott.

In 1879, L. M. Alcott sent a letter to *The Woman's Journal* regarding voting for school committee, and she signed it "Yours for reforms of all kinds." Reform was in Alcott's genes. Her parents endorsed most of the reforms of their day, from temperance to health food, from homeopathy to antislavery. Her father called woman suffrage the "reform of reforms." Her mother insisted that the "extension to woman of all civil rights" would enhance "the welfare and progress of the State." During the earlier part of her life, when she assumed the role of family breadwinner, Louisa Alcott was less mouthpiece of reform than she was wage earner. But at all times she supported her family's determination to amend what was wrong. She was aware of and often moved by the writings of others aimed at the reforms of their time, and in her own writings, especially in the domestic novels aimed at the young that poured from her pen, she aired her beliefs and prodded her readers to right the wrong.

Alcott's selection of reform measures to champion was wide indeed. It extended from reform at home to reform in the nation, from the classroom to the polling place. It is appropriate to begin

1

where she began—in her heart and in her masterpiece, *Little Women*—with the home and the domestic reforms embraced in nineteenth-century America.

In 1869, the year that Part Two of *Little Women* was published, introducing readers to one American home and catapulting its author to fame and fortune, a revised edition of a book entitled *The American Woman's Home* appeared in print. There is no doubt that Louisa Alcott was aware of it. She knew by reputation—as who did not?—the Beecher family. One of them had written *Uncle Tom's Cabin*, and the little woman who made the big war could find her work on Alcott's preferred list. By 1869, Harriet Beecher Stowe was a household name. Her half-sister was less universally recognized but no less of a crusader. Plain, heavy-featured, with lank hair, Catharine Beecher was an educator par excellence. Indeed, in 1866 she had taught briefly in Lexington, Massachusetts, at a school in which Alcott took a deep interest, Dio Lewis's school for girls. There were, as there would always be, connections between Louisa May Alcott and the printed sources that filtered into her life and work.

Even if *Little Women* had not portrayed one of the most cherished of American homes, its author would have been drawn to *The American Woman's Home* delineated by Catharine Beecher and Harriet Beecher Stowe. The American home had many aspects and was many things, though it was, as Alcott saw it, "a happy place, where parents and children, brothers and sisters, learn to love and know and help one another."

There is no doubt that the dinner table played a large and influential role in all American homes. Having often in early life subsisted largely on apples and brown bread, Alcott concurred with the Beechers in castigating intemperance in diet and advocating the "proper proportion of animal and vegetable food." The Beechers condemned "alcoholic drinks, opium mixtures, and tobacco," and, less vehemently, tea and coffee. Alcott agreed. She had suffered the effects of opiates after the illness she sustained as a Civil War nurse. With most of the health reformers of her time, she placed her faith in the beneficence of cold water.

If food and drink were the basics of life and of home, dress was also universally important. The great nineteenth-century reform in clothing was effected by opponents of tight-lacing whose vehemence against the confining corset was often tempestuous. The Beechers advocated "daily domestic exercise" in loose dresses, minus corsets and tight belts. Alcott was as ardent an anti-lacer as she was an anti-alcoholic.

Though she deviated upon occasion at her own table, yielding now and then to the pleasures of tea or coffee, she took care to incorporate the reformer's view with some consistency in her writings. The glories of brown bread and porridge and the superiority of new milk to coffee punctuate several lines in *Eight Cousins*. "Jimmy's Lecture," published as a press leaflet in the 1880s, is a forthright plea for temperance. As for clothing, in *An Old-Fashioned Girl* the author took occasion to laud "the good old fashion of simplicity," while in *Eight Cousins* the corset is denounced as "an instrument of torture," Dr. Alec declaiming: "Nature knows how to mould a woman better than any corset-maker."

Such domestic reforms warred long and persistently against nineteenth-century American intemperance in food and drink, fussiness and tight-lacing in clothing. Indeed, they became twentieth-century inheritances, and readers in the new century, scanning the Beechers' advice in *The American Woman's Home* or Alcott's hints in her still popular *Little Women* series, recognized the wrong being righted, the cause being cured. As domestic reformers, both the Beechers and Alcott were on the right track.

In the reform measures applied to other nineteenth-century health problems, Alcott and her mentors were somewhat less successful. Nineteenth-century America was rife with physical ills that needed curing, from those triggered by intemperance to such dire combinations as typhoid-pneumonia. The century was rife too with prescriptions that proved ineffective and with physicians who failed to heal. Both former and latter combatted disease with remedies that produced effects in direct opposition to the disease itself. In brief, they followed the medical practice known as allopathy. Its failings prompted the reforms that came to be known as alternative medicine. The Alcott family, stricken with smallpox during the summer of 1850, after Mrs. Alcott had fed some immigrants in the garden, joined the crusade against conservative medicine and turned to the practice called homeopathy.

Still debated today, homeopathy upheld several unusual precepts. Opposed to allopathy, it was based on the principle that "like cures like." A sick person can heal himself with tiny doses of medicine that produce the symptoms he already has. The emphasis here is on the adjective *tiny.* Any homeopathic medicine, nontoxic and derived from natural sources, is administered in excessively small amounts. The homeopathic system of "similars" was developed into a medical system by a German physician, Samuel Hahnemann, in the late 1700s, and the first American edition of his *Organon of the Healing Art* appeared in 1836. It was this work to which the Alcotts turned that devastating summer of 1850, and in it they found advice on medications and treatments, as well as an alternative to the accepted—a cudgel of reform.

Louisa Alcott not only remembered the details of the homeopathic system and practiced them periodically, but she also introduced them into her writings. In her "Lines to a Good Physician, From a Grateful Patient," she described the successful doctor as a source of comfort—the "Best of earthly physic/Bottled in a *friend."* Dr. Alec, her mouthpiece of reform in *Eight Cousins,* sends Rose's "regiment of bottles . . . smashing down into the posy-beds below."

While homeopathy was a reform prompted by traditional medical practice, another reform concept derived from and dominated the nineteenth-century science of the mind. This was phrenology, with its basic belief that the brain is the organ of the mind, that the brain is a congeries of organs and, concomitantly, that the mind is a congeries of faculties and character or temperament can be analyzed from an examination of the skull. Moreover, such phrenological character analyses could provide programs for self-improvement. "To Know Thyself" could be to improve thyself. Evil impulses could be eradicated. This view of human nature challenged the fatalists and intrigued the reformers who saw in it a shortcut to human perfectibility.

Louisa Alcott's philosopher-father experimented with phrenology in 1838 when Louisa herself was only six. For that purpose, he submitted his head to an examination by one of the Fowler brothers of New York, who were pioneering that new approach to character analysis.

In 1875, on a trip to New York, Louisa Alcott paid a visit to Fowler headquarters at 737 Broadway. There she entered a realm of busts, plaster casts, and skulls before seating herself for a phrenological examination. Her head was measured with a tape, and the examiner's exploring fingers made a tactile study of the areas in her skull that housed her faculties: her Amativeness and Friendship, her Benevolence and Ideality. Although the phrenologist erred in calling her a "devoted wife & mother," he deduced the "dual nature" of the author of the domestic *Little Women* and the sensational *Behind a Mask*. Most of her faculties the examiner found unusually large, and he classified her head as "remarkable."

Louisa made a manuscript copy of the analysis and inserted it into the handbook she acquired at the Phrenological Depot, *How to Read Character*. On January 1, 1876, she presented the volume to her older sister, Anna Pratt, inscribing a ditty "To Nan" on the first flyleaf. The verses recalled a phrenological doll from days when phrenological fervor extended even to the nursery.

As late as the 1880s, a phrenological analysis based upon a portrait of Louisa May Alcott appeared in the *Phrenological Journal*, but by the turn of the century the zeal of phrenological reform died out. The twentieth century obliterated many of the certainties and affirmations of the nineteenth, and later reformers, questioning the relationship of skull and brain, organ and faculties, cast doubts upon the perfectibility of man.

Alcott experimented less satisfactorily with yet another health-related reform, one that was based on the conviction that mind and body were inextricably interrelated. Mary Baker Eddy, with whom Bronson Alcott corresponded, had published her revolutionary *Science and Health* in 1875, introducing Christian Science to a world weary of physicking. Tenuously related to that approach to illness was another approach known by the 1880s as mind cure. It too was one of the reforms of the age, akin in some measure to hygienic dress and temperance, a cause to venture, an aspect of the newness. Louisa Alcott turned to it, seeking relief for physical ills and sponsoring a health reform.

Mind cure would prove no panacea for Alcott or for an ailing world. At first, however, it seemed to one sufferer "very wonderful." When, early in 1885, she was plagued with vertigo, rheumatism of the right arm, and an ache at the back of her head, Alcott enlisted the aid of a healer named Anna B. Newman with an office at 17 Boylston Place, Boston. There they sat together in complete silence for fifteen minutes, until Louisa, eyes closed, felt a stillness, a lightness, a "floating away on a sea of rest." Once or twice, she "seemed to have no body, & to come back from another world. I felt as if I trod on air & was very happy & young for some hours."

Mrs. Newman had induced such sensations by means of a remarkable psychical treatment. She listened to her patient's complaints and observations, and as she listened she mentally denied every symptom mentioned, selected one in particular for healing, and silently directed her will against the error and her patient's false belief in error. The silent treatment was followed by cheerful conversation and repeated assurances of the infinite power of mind.

Alcott enjoyed her early reactions—the sense of "sunshine in the head," the "slight trances"—but her receptive, passive state proved evanescent while her rheumatism and headache proved persistent. She began to doubt a reform that claimed "to cure cancers, yet could not help a headache," and returned instead to homeopathy and massage.

At the end of 1882, Anna B. Newman had delivered an address before the Woman's Educational and Industrial Union in Boston, elaborating mind cure's basic concept that "the physical nature is only the . . . shadow of mind." By the spring of 1885, Alcott reported her experience with the revolutionary treatment to *The Woman's Journal,* concluding that in her case it had failed and labeling it not a new reform but a "new craze." It would seem to be the fate of many psychological approaches to medicine. Mind cure, combining some of the tenets of Christian Science and psychoanalysis, was certainly a reform in its day, or at least an attempted reform.

If the nineteenth-century reforms that centered on health have not all been long-lasting, most of the reforms leveled at the philosophy and practice of education have endured. For this, the work of three people close to Louisa Alcott is in some measure responsible. Much might be said of a derogatory nature about Bronson Alcott as a family man who could not support his family, but the revolutionary ideas he advanced as father and as teacher had a beneficent effect and survived. He sought especially to reform the ingrained nineteenth-century educational practice of stuffing young minds with undigested information; he encouraged instead the self-expression of youth, drawing his pupils out, spurring them to articulate their own thoughts, their own feelings. This was an ultra-modern pedagogical method that Bronson Alcott pursued, both at his Temple School in Boston, opened in the fall of 1834, and at home with his own children.

One of his teachers at the school, Elizabeth Palmer Peabody, not only shared Alcott's experimental reforms in education, but recorded them in her *Record of a School,* published in 1835. There she wrote: "it would hardly be believed what an evident exercise it was to the children, to be led of themselves to form and express these conceptions and few steps of reasoning. Every face was eager and interested." Education at the Temple School adhered literally to its Latin derivation—it was a drawing out.

The same year that *Record of a School* was published, on November 29 Louisa marked her third birthday at that school in a joint celebration with her father, who turned thirty-six. Probably for the first time she saw the rooms at the top of the Temple where educational reform was being attempted: the busts of learned men, the figure of Silence, the globes and slates, the blocks and books. She would not forget the experience. Her father's pedagogical innovations would one day be converted into literary source material.

Some years later, starting in May 1859, Bronson Alcott was appointed superintendent of Concord Schools for a six-year term. The principles he had applied both in the Temple School and at home were applied now to a wider area. They are reflected in the school reports he wrote, reports based upon the innovative belief that "Every child feels early the desire for communicating his emotions and thoughts, first by conversation and next by writing." Louisa concurred, and in her father's school exhibition of 1861 she participated in a minor way by writing the words to a song.

Despite the war, Concord was a fertile field for educational reform in the 1860s. Another innovator encouraged by Bronson Alcott was Dr. Dio Lewis, a temperance reformer and pioneer in gymnastic education. In 1864 this rotund enthusiast purchased a large summer hotel at nearby Lexington, which he converted into a background for pedagogical experimentation. It was an experiment that Louisa Alcott observed with close attention. In Dr. Dio Lewis's Lexington seminary, young ladies in gymnastic costumes exercised with clubs and beanbags and followed his gospel of plain food, strong shoes, and early hours. Louisa Alcott imbibed enough of his educational reforms to interweave them into her tales. Both her father's methods of letting the mind unfold and Dr. Lewis's musical gymnastics would reappear in her fiction.

When Alcott converted the Temple School into the Plumfield of *Little Men,* she took many of her words out of her father's mouth, but gave them a different accent. As Jo March Bhaer remarks, "little minds" are cultivated not with "long, hard lessons, parrot-learned," but by "helping [them] to unfold." And again: "Boys at other schools probably learned more from books, but less of that better wisdom which makes good men." The educational reform she had witnessed pops up in *An Old-Fashioned Girl* and *Eight Cousins.* The evil of cramming "pupils like Thanksgiving turkeys" is deplored, and "feeding them in a natural and wholesome way" endorsed. By the time she came to write the last of the *Little Women* series, *Jo's Boys,* Alcott envisioned her Laurence College as an institution that "believed . . . heartily in the right of all sexes, colors, creeds, and ranks in education." In her pedagogical credo, the reforms she had observed in Boston and Concord were universalized.

In *Jo's Boys,* too, she remarked that education "is not confined to books." Amused as she might have been by Dr. Lewis's new gymnastics—"every one has become a perambulating windmill with all four sails going"—she joined the pioneers and produced a serial on the subject for the Concord *Monitor* in 1862, entitled "The King of Clubs and the Queen of Hearts." This tale of a New England experiment she subtitled "A Story for Young America." There is no doubt that young America ardently embraced the educational reform it described.

Bronson Alcott introduced his daughter not only to the newness in education, but to the newness in American social life. With the majority of Americans, she applauded the former but disavowed the latter. She looked upon the communal societies that peppered the nineteenth-century landscape with a tongue-in-cheek attitude as she scanned the idiosyncrasies of their reformer denizens.

On June 1, 1843, when Louisa was ten years old, the family moved to a dilapidated building on Prospect Hill in Harvard, Massachusetts. The radical British thinker and reformer Charles Lane, who had invited Bronson Alcott to visit another "Temple School" in England, paid Alcott's debts and purchased the Wyman Farm in Harvard. Now, with Lane and his son William, the Alcott family would metamorphose itself into a Consociate Family. Shortly after their arrival, Bronson Alcott described his intentions glowingly in a letter to his brother Junius: "This dell is the canvas on which I will paint a picture . . . a worthy picture for mankind." He called that dell Fruitlands and conceived it as a new Eden.

It was certainly new. As Emerson observed during a summer visit, in July it looked well—he would see it in December. Charles Lane planned to dispense with the plow in favor of handwork with spade and pruning knife. Bronson Alcott sought to enter the kingdom of peace through the gates of denial. Linen tunics were the only permissible garments, since cotton would encourage slavery and wool would deprive the sheep of its natural clothing. A bloodless diet depended heavily on fruits and fountain waters. The idiosyncratic reforms increased as the Consociate Family expanded. One refused to drink milk that rightly belonged to the cow. Another secreted cheese in a trunk. Charles Lane, supervising the children's lessons, recorded a long list of Louisa's vices, ranging from impatience to impudence. Tensions developed among the Consociate Family as well as in the Alcott family. After six months in New Eden they abandoned Fruitlands and moved to Still River.

Fruitlands, of course, was only one of many communal societies designed to reform a conventional modus vivendi. Near Prospect Hill a Shaker community prospered under the communism of labor and property. Brook Farm in West Roxbury, Massachusetts, developed an association devoted less to dietary restriction than to intellectual expansion. Nineteenth-century America was a fertile field for experimental communities: Modern Times and the Oneida Community in New York State, New Harmony in Indiana. Such communal societies as these sprang up across the country, each aimed at one or another societal reform, and all of them aimed at Utopia.

Louisa Alcott, who had experienced one such experiment, recorded her reactions to the newness of consociate living twice: the first at the time of the experience, in her journal; the second thirty years later, in a semifictional article for the *Independent*. Her journal tells us briefly of her life at Fruitlands: her work, her thoughts, her reading. "We had a dinner of bread and water after which I read thought and walked till supper. . . . Anna and I did the work. In the evening Mr. Lane asked us, 'What is man?' . . . After a long talk we went to bed very tired. . . . Anna and I had a long talk. I was very unhappy, and we all cried. Anna and I cried in bed, and I prayed God to keep us all together."

In "Transcendental Wild Oats," written for *The Independent*, Alcott made light of much of the poverty and dreariness of Fruitlands. By 1873, time had healed the wounds of an experiment that had been tried and found wanting. Now, glossing over the past, she used the experience to clear her own mind and satisfy the unceasing demands of an ever-increasing readership. She introduced the "prospective Eden" as consisting of "an old red farm-house, a dilapidated barn, many acres of meadow-land, and a grove," christened Fruitlands by its "sanguine founders." Intended as "a colony of Latter Day Saints," it would "regenerate the world." Exaggerating the unrealistic ambitions of the Consociate Brotherhood, Alcott painted a lighthearted but basically factual account of their way of life. Their diet consisted of "unleavened bread, porridge, and water for breakfast; bread, vegetables, and water for dinner; bread, fruit, and water for supper. . . . No teapot profaned that sacred stove, no gory steak cried aloud for vengeance . . . and only a brave woman's taste, time, and temper were sacrificed on that domestic altar." The brethren were described laughingly along with their linen dress, vegetarian tastes, and the "reform conventions" of those "who said many wise things and did many foolish ones." The ill-fated and misnamed society of Fruitlands was rechristened Apple Slump, and Alcott, looking back in sadness and wry amusement, rescattered for her public the "Transcendental Wild Oats" that had been sown in 1843.

By the 1850s, when the family had moved to Boston, a reform far more universal and far more incendiary than communal society was gathering strength. In this case Louisa Alcott was a powerful participant. Her identification with the antislavery cause was part of her inheritance. All the Alcotts were antislavery. It was her cousin Samuel Sewall who defended the fugitive slave Thomas Sims, a man guilty of no crime except the love of liberty. In her 1851 journal, the nineteen-year-old Louisa wrote: "I felt ready to do anything,—fight or work, hoot or cry,—and laid plans to free Simms. I shall be horribly ashamed of my country if this thing happens and the slave is taken back." Years later she added a note: "He was."

In 1854, the return of another fugitive slave affected Alcott even more deeply. Anthony Burns had fled Richmond in February; on May 24 he was arrested in Boston, and "the excitement . . . during the following week was said to have been without parallel since the days of the Revolution." Bronson Alcott joined with members of the Vigilance Committee to rescue the fugitive from the courthouse, but the attempt failed, and on June 2 Burns was returned to his owner. As she stood on Boston's Court Square, Alcott saw the houses draped in black, the crowds on the sidewalks hissing the troops, the flags waving Union down. For a moment she caught a glimpse of the fugitive's face, scarred by a burn or a brand. She would not forget the rendition of Anthony Burns, or his scar. She would fight the antislavery fight in her own way, and in her fiction make use of a comparable scar.

The ferociously debated questions of the day were surely coming to open war. By May 1859, Captain John Brown—Osawatomie Brown—was speaking on Kansas affairs at Concord Town Hall. As he discussed his invasion of Missouri, he seemed to Alcott a dauntless figure, tall and imposing, ready to face a hostile world. In October the news arrived: John Brown had entered Harpers Ferry, liberated the slaves, and with his small force held the town for thirty hours. His deeds were applauded by some, condemned by others, but even residents of Harpers Ferry who deplored the actions of an abolitionist fanatic took pains to describe them graphically. In his own speech before the court John Brown insisted that what he had done was right, and before his death sentence was carried out he reminded his listeners: "You may dispose of me very easily; . . . but this question is still to be settled . . . the end of that is not yet."

On December 2, John Brown was executed. Alcott's reaction was expressed in a poem that interpreted that execution as martyrdom and his deed as a "flower, In the wilderness of wrong." The Alcotts welcomed members of John Brown's family to their home as they had welcomed John Brown to the life of the nation. In April 1861 Alcott wrote in her journal: "War declared with the South, . . . I've often longed to see a war, and now I have my wish. I long to be a man, but as I can't fight, I will content myself with working for those who can."

In November 1862 Alcott applied for a post as army nurse in Washington. She was accepted in December and assigned to the Union Hotel Hospital in Georgetown, where Matron Hannah Ropes initiated her in her duties. She became acquainted with brown soap and bedpans, with nurses who sang hymns while they stole money, with doctors and with patients. Her stay at the Union Hotel Hospital would be a short one, running from December 13 to January 24, cut short by a serious illness that necessitated her return home. But during that brief period she became familiar not only with the joy of working for a great cause, but with the battles that cause engendered—Fredericksburg and Antietam—that loosed their victims into the Union Hotel Hospital. From this ordeal, part of the severest ordeal in American history, Louisa Alcott emerged with a grave illness labeled typhoid-pneumonia, with unforgettable memories, and with material for a book.

Hospital Sketches, published in 1863 by the abolitionist James Redpath, recalled the nurses and doctors, the sponges, the basins and bandages, but it also recalled the trials of wounded men, the fate of soldiers in a civil war. The book touched the hearts of those who followed the experiences of "Nurse Tribulation Periwinkle," and the critics were enthusiastic, grateful for the author's "touches of quiet humor" and "graphically drawn" scenes. Alcott had given much of herself to the antislavery reform that culminated in civil war, but she had taken from it a book that would become a perennial reminder of her experience.

Until another book transformed Alcott's life, the author was constantly aware of economic struggle. The hardships involved in sustaining a family formed an obbligato to her days before the publication in 1868–1869 of the universally popular *Little Women*. With a philosopher father who seemed incapable of amassing or even earning sufficient money, Louisa took upon herself the role of family breadwinner. It was a role that constantly alerted her to the occupational limitations of nineteenth-century American women. They could follow teaching, as she did upon several occasions; they could be seamstresses, as she was from time to time; they could be nurses; and they could enter domestic service. Alcott did that too in the winter of 1851, and found it a chastening experience. To all her fund-raising activities, writing formed a background.

There is little doubt that, as she tried one occupation after another, Louisa Alcott was aware of one writer's views on the subject. *Woman in the Nineteenth Century* had first appeared in 1845, the work of Margaret Fuller, whom Alcott recalled from her father's Temple School. After Elizabeth Peabody had departed, Margaret Fuller took her place there. On a visit to the Alcott home, the learned Miss Fuller announced that she had come to see the "model children," whose horseplay failed to fill the description. Margaret Fuller had been a fleeting figure in Louisa's early years, but after her death in 1850, her book restored her to memory. In its pages Alcott, experiencing the limitations of woman's economic role, read the following explosive exhortation: "We would have every arbitrary barrier thrown down. We would have every path laid open to woman as freely as to man. . . . if you ask me what offices they may fill; I reply—any. I do not care what case you put; let them be sea-captains, if you will."

Alcott was never a sea captain. She did not pioneer in opening untraditional offices to women. What she did do was assume the economic role of provider for a family, and in so doing she practised the egalitarianism that others preached. Egalitarianism was a natural concomitant of expanding the occupational opportunities available to women. Those who preached that expansion included Alcott's mother—"Open to women a great variety of employments"—and a friend of her later years, Dr. Marie Zakrzewska. That pioneer physician founded the New England Hospital for Women and Children, where an Alcott relative, Lucy Sewall, became resident physician. The hospital would engage Alcott's support, and "Dr. Z." would appear in an Alcott story.

Alcott habitually wove into her fiction not only the characters of people she had known, but the views she upheld. The "trials of young women who want employment & find it hard to get" appear and reappear, not only in her letters but in such stories as "How I Went Out to Service." In "Happy Women," she describes the work of four women: one was undoubtedly based upon the career of Dr. Lucy Sewall as "resident physician of a city hospital"; another was based upon her own experience.

It is in the autobiographical novel *Work* (first called "Success"), published in 1873, that Alcott addresses herself most expansively to the subject of woman's economic role. There her protagonist, Christie Devon, becomes companion, seamstress, servant, and actress, following the efforts of Alcott herself. *Work* is accurately subtitled *A Story of Experience*. The limitations of the employments sketched were the limitations of life.

In the extension of economic opportunity for women Alcott saw the consequence of egalitarianism. In a letter of 1874 she expressed the hope that the high school headmaster's salary would be reduced and that of the first woman assistant increased "to make the pay equal. I believe in the same pay for the same good work." And she added: "let woman do whatever she can do; let men place no more impediments in the way; . . . let *simple justice* be done." In *Rose in Bloom,* her heroine reiterates, "It is as much a right and a duty for women to do something with their lives as for men." "Let us hear no more of 'woman's sphere,' " she wrote in her 1874 letter, "either from our . . . legislators beneath the State House dome, or from our clergymen in their pulpits." Though she never opened up a restricted or prohibited profession to women, Alcott assuredly pioneered in trying to abolish "woman's sphere."

Throughout her lifetime, however, the concept of woman's sphere remained inviolate to the conventional majority. Even the progres-

sive William Andrus Alcott, Bronson's cousin, who wrote so profusely about human relations, offered advice less revolutionary than
traditional in his volume *The Young Wife*. Margaret Fuller, of course,
told another story. She did not fear to explore the nature of androgyny: "Male and female represent the two sides of the great radical
dualism. But, in fact, they are perpetually passing into one another.
Fluid hardens to solid, solid rushes to fluid. There is no wholly masculine man, no purely feminine woman." As for egalitarianism, Fuller went beyond—to independence. "That her hand may be given
with dignity, she must be able to stand alone." And as for marriage,
she was equally outspoken: "A profound thinker has said, 'no married woman can represent the female world, for she belongs to her
husband. The idea of woman must be represented by a virgin.' But
that is the very fault of marriage, and of the present relation between
the sexes, that the woman does belong to the man, instead of forming a whole with him."

Egalitarianism, independence, androgyny, sexual harmony—all
were part of nineteenth-century feminism. And Louisa May Alcott
proceeded to blend all those elements into the fabric of what is perhaps her strongest feminist narrative. Struggling to pay family bills
by exercising her skill in sensational storytelling, she recorded in her
December 1866 journal: "Wrote . . . a wild Russian story 'Taming a
Tartar.' "

Her hero, the savage, swarthy, tyrannical Russian Prince Alexis,
is male chauvinism personified. Her heroine, Sybil Varna, a former
English teacher in a girls' "pensionnat," engages him in a mighty
sexual power struggle that ends only when she has tamed the Tartar.
The rounds of that struggle, won by heroine Sybil, are the episodes
of the story. "I was bent on having my own way," she confesses,
"and making him submit as a penance for his unwomanly menace.
Once conquer his will, . . . and I had gained a power possessed by
no other person. I liked the trial." The finale would satisfy the most
ardent feminist. Alexis remarks, "I might boast that I also had tamed
a fiery spirit, but I am humble, and content myself with the knowledge that the proudest woman ever born has promised to love,
honor, and—" at which Sybil breaks in quickly with "*Not* obey
you."

"Taming a Tartar" appeared as an anonymous four-part serial in 1867. Some years later, Louisa M. Alcott signed her name to a letter articulating her boldly feminist view of a nonfictional event. The letter was dispatched to *The Woman's Journal*, which published it in 1875 as "Woman's Part in the Concord Celebration." A description of the Concord celebration of the nation's centennial on April 19, that letter was in reality a clarion call to the future. While streams of men gathered at the pavilion on the Provincial Parade, the women had to assemble at Town Hall, waiting to be conducted to the Oration Tent. Thus began the town's gala festivities in which hospitalities were extended only to the men. Forced to wait for an escort that never arrived, the ladies charged into a tent pitched for the occasion, but found no room on a platform reserved for men. Women were given no opportunity to participate in honoring their country until the marine band struck up at the evening ball. In Concord's desire to exalt the heroes of old, the village had forgotten the heroines of the present. Another protest was required, and Alcott was ready. She ended "Woman's Part in the Concord Celebration" on a trumpet note: "there will come a day of reckoning, and then the tax-paying women of Concord will not be forgotten . . . *then,* . . . following in the footsteps of their forefathers, [women] will utter another protest that shall be 'heard round the world.' "

Alcott was well aware that in the United States of America the clearest path to protest was paved with the right to vote. She wrote to her publisher, Thomas Niles of Roberts Brothers, in 1881: "I can remember when Anti slavery was in just the same state that Suffrage is now, and take more pride in the very small help we Alcotts could give than in all the books I ever wrote or ever shall write."

The Alcotts were as ardently prosuffrage as they had been antislavery. Louisa's mother had petitioned the citizens of Massachusetts on equal political rights of woman; her father defined woman suffrage as the "reform of reforms." She could endorse William Henry Channing's championship of woman suffrage in 1853 only as an inalienable right: "constituting one-half of the people of these free and United States, . . . [free women are entitled] to possess and use the power of voting, now monopolized by that other half of the people, the free men."

Alcott's active participation in the woman suffrage movement took on force in the mid-1870s. In 1873 she declared herself "so busy just now proving 'Woman's Right to Labor' that I have no time to help prove 'Woman's Right to Vote.' " As the years passed, however, she did take time. She held suffrage meetings at her home in an attempt to stir up the apathetic women of Concord. When the right to vote for school committee was granted to Concord's taxpaying women, Alcott was the "first woman to register my name as a voter."

Alcott's zeal for woman suffrage is best reflected in her letters— letters sent to that leading suffragist, Lucy Stone, to *The Woman's Journal,* the only woman suffrage paper published in Massachusetts, and to the American Woman Suffrage Association. In them she registered her disappointments and her hopes, especially her hopes for the future: "as the conservative elders pass away, the new generation will care less for the traditions of the past, more for the work of the present, and taking a brave part in it, will add fresh honors to the fine old town, which should be marching abreast with the foremost, not degenerating into a museum for revolutionary relics, or a happy hunting-ground for celebrity-seekers." In her 1885 letter to the American Woman Suffrage Association, the woman who had once signed herself, "Yours for reforms of all kinds," now placed woman suffrage in the lead. "After a fifty years' acquaintance with the noble men and women of the anti-slavery cause . . . I should be a traitor to all I most love, honor and desire to imitate if I did not covet a place among those who are giving their lives to the emancipation of the white slaves of America." That letter she signed, "Most heartily yours for woman suffrage and all other reforms." And in Alcott's last novel of her *Little Women* series, *Jo's Boys,* a play, *The Owlsdark Marbles,* is performed at Plumfield. One of those "Marbles" embodies the goddess Minerva, whose shield is adorned with the words "Women's Rights."

Especially during the latter half of the nineteenth century, the persistence of many wrongs propelled crusades to right them. To domestic reform and alternative medicine, to education and communal society, to antislavery and egalitarianism, to feminism and suffrage, L. M. Alcott at one time or another, in one way or another, lent her signature of reform. It appears in her actions and in her books, the sign of a human being impatient with indifference, apathy, and intolerance. Louisa Alcott's advocacy was a firm and convincing one that advanced many causes while it enriched her life.

This book is the outcome of two innovative and significant conversational series held in 2000 and 2001 at the Orchard House, home of the Alcotts, in Concord, Massachusetts. The first series was based upon Alcott's sign-off, "Yours for reforms of all kinds," and it set the theme of a workshop, a film series, and lectures. The theme continued in the conversational series of 2001, "Life Is My College," Concord's College of Education.

Both series were organized by the dynamic director of the Orchard House, Jan Turnquist, and her Director of Education, Sheryl Peters. The workshop, film series, lectures, and presentations were conducted by noted scholars led by Professor Sarah Elbert: Melissa Pennell, Dan Shealy, Ronald Bosco, Cynthia Barton, Jayne Gordon, Michael Pierson, Kate Henchman, and others. On each occasion participants received "a resource binder of primary source material for classroom use." It was the binder I received in connection with the summer conversational series of 2000 that prompted me to shape this book. As I leafed through the fairly voluminous collection of writings by nineteenth-century American reformers and by L. M. Alcott herself, my reaction was: There could be a book here that would be of interest not only to Alcott enthusiasts but to the general public. In it they would find reflected much about nineteenth-century American life and society: its ills and its attempted cures, as well as the reactions of America's best-loved writer of juvenile stories. Louisa May Alcott, who was memorialized as the Children's Friend, was also adept at the blood and thunder of sensation fiction. Now it is clear that she was, in addition, a woman who saw what was wrong and tried to right it, a woman who pledged herself "Yours for reforms of all kinds."

It is that woman who dominates this book, along with the reforms she endorsed and the reformers she supported. Here the Alcott signature becomes the Signature of Reform.

1

Domestic Reform: Food, Drink, Dress

The American Woman's Home

(1869; Revision of Catharine Beecher's
A Treatise on Domestic Economy, 1841)

CATHARINE BEECHER AND
HARRIET BEECHER STOWE

IX. HEALTHFUL FOOD.

The person who decides what shall be the food and drink of a family, and the modes of its preparation, is the one who decides, to a greater or less extent, what shall be the health of that family. It is the opinion of most medical men, that intemperance in eating is one of the most fruitful of all causes of disease and death. If this be so, the woman who wisely adapts the food and cooking of her family to the laws of health removes one of the greatest risks which threatens the lives of those under her care. But, unfortunately, there is no other duty that has been involved in more doubt and perplexity. Were one to believe all that is said and written on this subject, the conclusion probably would be, that there is not one solitary article of food on God's earth which it is healthful to eat. Happily, however, there are general principles on this subject which, if understood and applied, will prove a safe guide to any woman of common sense; and it is the object of the following chapter to set forth these principles. . . .

Experiments on animals prove that fine flour alone, which is chiefly carbon, will not sustain life more than a month, while unbolted flour furnishes all that is needed for every part of the body. There are cases where persons can not use such coarse bread, on account of its irritating action on inflamed coats of the stomach. For such, a kind of wheaten grit is provided, containing all the kernel of the wheat, except the outside woody fibre. . . .

The proper digestion of food depends on the wants of the body, and on its power of appropriating the aliment supplied. The best of food can not be properly digested when it is not needed. All that the system requires will be used, and the rest will be thrown out by the several excreting organs, which thus are frequently over-taxed, and vital forces are wasted. Even food of poor quality may digest well if the demands of the system are urgent. The way to increase digestive power is to increase the demand for food by pure air and exercise of the muscles, quickening the blood, and arousing the whole system to a more rapid and vigorous rate of life. . . .

Students who need food with little carbon, and women who live in the house, should always seek coarse bread; fruits, and lean meats, and avoid butter, oils, sugar, and molasses, and articles containing them.

Many students and women using little exercise in the open air, grow thin and weak, because the vital powers are exhausted in throwing off excess of food, especially of the carbonaceous. . . .

When too great a supply of food is put into the stomach, the gastric juice dissolves only that portion which the wants of the system demand. Much of the remainder is ejected, in an unprepared state. . . . Very often, intemperance in eating produces immediate results, such as colic, headaches, pains of indigestion, and vertigo. . . .

The general rule, then, is, that three hours be given to the stomach for labor, and two for rest; and in obedience to this, five hours, at least, ought to elapse between every two regular meals. In cases where exercise produces a flow of perspiration, more food is needed to supply the loss; and strong laboring men may safely eat as often as they feel the want of food. So, young and healthy children, who gambol and exercise much and whose bodies grow fast, may have a more frequent supply of food. But, as a general rule, meals should be five hours apart, and eating between meals avoided. There is nothing more unsafe, and wearing to the constitution, than a habit of eating at any time merely to gratify the palate. . . .

Those persons who keep their bodies in a state of health by sufficient exercise can always be guided by the calls of hunger. They can eat when they feel hungry, and stop when hunger ceases; and thus they will calculate exactly right. But the difficulty is, that a large part of the community, especially women, are so inactive in their habits that they seldom feel the calls of hunger. They habitually eat, merely to gratify the palate. . . .

It is also found, by experience, that the lean part of animal food is more stimulating than vegetable. This is the reason why, in cases of fevers or inflammations, medical men forbid the use of meat. A person who lives chiefly on animal food is under a higher degree of stimulus than if his food was chiefly composed of vegetable substances. His blood will flow faster, and all the functions of his body will be quickened. This makes it important to secure a proper proportion of animal and vegetable diet. Some medical men suppose that an exclusively vegetable diet is proved, by the experience of many individuals, to be fully sufficient to nourish the body. . . . in America, far too large a portion of the diet consists of animal food.

X. HEALTHFUL DRINKS.

In this country there are three forms in which the use of . . . stimulants is common; namely *alcoholic drinks, opium mixtures,* and *tobacco.* These are all alike in the main peculiarity of imparting that extra stimulus to the system which tends to exhaust its powers. . . . When alcohol is taken into the stomach, . . . it is always carried to the brain. The consequence is, that it affects that nature and action of the brain-cells, until a habit is formed which is *automatic;* that is, the mind loses the power of controlling the brain in its development of thoughts, feelings, and choices as it would in the natural state, and is itself controlled by the brain. In this condition a real disease of the brain is created, called *vino-mania,* (or wine-madness,) and the only remedy is total abstinence, and that for a long period, from the alcoholic poison. . . .

It is allowed by all medical men that pure water is perfectly healthful and supplies all the liquid needed by the body; and also that by proper means, which ordinarily are in the reach of all, water can be made sufficiently pure.

It is allowed by all that milk, and the juices of fruits, when taken into the stomach, furnish water that is always pure and that our bread and vegetable food also supply it in large quantities. There are besides a great variety of agreeable and healthful beverages, made from the juices of fruit, containing no alcohol, and agreeable drinks, such as milk, cocoa, and chocolate, that contain no stimulating principles, and which are nourishing and healthful.

As one course, then, is perfectly safe and another involves great danger, it is wrong and sinful to choose the path of danger. There is no peril in drinking pure water, milk, the juices of fruits, and infusions that are nourishing and harmless. But there is great danger to the young, and to the commonwealth, in patronizing the sale and use of alcoholic drinks. . . . Tea has not one particle of nourishing properties; and what little exists in the coffee-berry is lost by roasting it in the usual mode. All that these articles do, is simply *to stimulate without nourishing.* . . .

The use of opium, especially by women, is usually caused at first by medical prescriptions containing it. All that has been stated as to the effect of alcohol in the brain is true of opium; while, to break a habit thus induced is almost hopeless. Every woman who takes or who administers this drug, is dealing as with poisoned arrows, whose wounds are without cure.

XII. CLOTHING.

The compression of the lower part of the waist is especially dangerous at the time young girls first enter society and are tempted to dress according to the fashion. Many a school-girl, whose waist was originally of a proper and healthful size, has gradually pressed the soft bones of youth until the lower ribs that should rise and fall with every breath, become entirely unused. . . . No stiff bone should be allowed to press in front, and the jacket should be so loose that a full breath can be inspired with ease, while in a sitting position. . . .

If a school-girl dress without corsets and without tight belts could be established as a fashion, it would be one step gained in the right direction. Then if mothers could secure daily domestic exercise in chambers, eating-rooms and parlors in loose dresses, a still farther advance would be secured.

L. M. Alcott's Domestic Philosophy

(*Merry's Museum*, October 1869)

The "Old-Fashioned Girl" is not intended as a period model, but as a possible improvement upon the Girl of the Period, who seems sorrowfully ignorant or ashamed of the good old fashions which make woman truly beautiful and honored, and, through her, render home what it should be,—a happy place, where parents and children, brothers and sisters, learn to love and know and help one another.

L. M. Alcott on Food

(*Eight Cousins*, 1875)

When her uncle appeared at sound of the bell, he found her survey-ing with an anxious face a new dish that smoked upon the table.

"Got a fresh trouble, Rosy?" he asked, stroking her smooth head.

"Uncle, *are* you going to make me eat oatmeal?" asked Rose, in tragic tone.

"Don't you like it?"

"I de-test it!" answered Rose, with all the emphasis which a turned-up nose, a shudder, and a groan could give to the three words.

"You are not a true Scotchwoman, if you don't like the 'parritch.' It's a pity, for I made it myself, and thought we'd have such a good time with all that cream to float in it. Well, never mind." And he sat down with a disappointed air.

Rose had made up her mind to be obstinate about it, because she did heartily "detest" the dish, but as Uncle Alec did not attempt to make her obey, she suddenly changed her mind and thought she would.

"I'll try to eat it to please you, uncle; but people are always saying how wholesome it is, and that makes me hate it," she said, half ashamed at her silly excuse.

"I do want you to like it, because I wish my girl to be as well and strong as Jessie's boys, who are brought up on this in the good old fashion. No hot bread and fried stuff for them, and they are the big-gest and bonniest lads of the lot."

. . . Phebe came out of the dining-room with a plate of brown bread, for Rose had been allowed no biscuit for tea.

". . . I'd rather you learned how to make good bread than the best pies ever baked. When you bring me a handsome, wholesome loaf, entirely made by yourself, I shall be more pleased than if you offered me a pair of slippers embroidered in the very latest style. I'll . . . promise to eat every crumb of the loaf myself."

It was some time before the perfect loaf appeared, for bread-making is an art not easily learned, . . . so Rose studied yeast first, and . . . came at last to the crowning glory of the "handsome, wholesome loaf."

L. M. Alcott on Drink

(Eight Cousins, 1875)

[Dr. Alec] smiled . . . as he said,—"This is part of the cure, Rose, and I put you here that you might take my three great remedies in the best and easiest way. Plenty of sun, fresh air, and cold water."

Phebe appeared with a cup of coffee.

"Debby told me to bring this and help you get up," she said. . . .

"I'm all dressed, so I don't need any help. I hope that is good and strong," added Rose, eyeing the steaming cup with an eager look.

But she did not get it, for a brown hand took possession of it as her uncle said quickly,—

"Hold hard, my lass, and let me overhaul that dose before you take it. Do you drink all this strong coffee every morning, Rose?"

"Yes, sir, and I like it. Auntie says it 'tones' me up, and I always feel better after it."

"This accounts for the sleepless nights, the flutter your heart gets into at the least start, and this is why that cheek of yours is pale yellow instead of rose red. No more coffee for you, my dear, and by and by you'll see that I am right. Any new milk downstairs, Phebe?"

"Yes, sir, plenty—right in from the barn."

"That's the drink for my patient. Go bring me a pitcherfull, and another cup; I want a draught myself."

L. M. Alcott on Drink

("Jimmy's Lecture," from *The Union Signal*;
The Press Leaflets, 1887?)

"Jimmy, throw that jug into the pig-pen. Smash it first, and be sure you don't taste a drop of the vile stuff," said an anxious-looking woman as she handed her little son the brown jug which she had just found hidden in the shed.

"Father won't like it," began the boy, eyeing the ugly thing with a look of fear and hate; for it made mother miserable, and father a brute.

"I said I'd make way with it the next time I found it, and I will! It's full, and I don't feel as if I could live through another dreadful time like the last. If we put it out of sight, maybe father will keep sober for another month. Be quick, before he comes home." And the poor woman pushed the boy to the door as if she could not wait a minute till the curse of her life was destroyed.

Glad to comfort her, and have the fun of smashing anything, Jimmy ran off, and giving the jug a good bang on the post, let the whiskey run where it would as he flung the pieces into the pig-pen, and went back to his work.

He was only eleven; but he struggled manfully with the old saw, and the tough apple-tree boughs he had collected for fuel. It was father's work, but he neglected it, and Jimmy wouldn't see mother suffer from cold, so he trimmed the trees, and did his best to keep the fire going. He had to stop often to rest, and in these pauses he talked to himself, having no other company.

Not long after the destruction of the jug, he heard a great commotion in the pen, and, looking in, saw the two pigs capering about in a curious way. Then ran up and down, squealed and skipped, and bumped against one another as if they didn't see straight, and had no control of their legs.

Jimmy was much amused for a few minutes, but, when one staggered to the trough, and began to lap something there, and the other tumbled down and could not get up, he understood the cause of these antics.

"Orchard House, dear! I let the whiskey run into the trough, and those bad pigs are tipsy! What shall I do?"

He watched them an instant, and then added in a sober tone, as he shook his head sadly, "That's just the way father does, lively first, then cross, then stupid. They don't look funny to me now, and I'm so sorry for 'em. They will be dreadfully ashamed when they get sober. I'm glad there isn't any wife and little son to be scared and mortified and sorry over 'em. I'll talk to 'em, and tell 'em what the man said in the temperance lecture we went to last night. Maybe it will do 'em good."

So Jimmy mounted the chopping-block close by, and repeated all he could remember, making a funny jumble, but being very much in earnest, and quite unconscious that he had another hearer beside the pigs:—

"My friends, rum is an awful thing. People who drink are slaves. They are worse than dumb beasts who don't drink. (Yes, they do; but that was my fault.) Half the sin and sorrow in the world come from rum. Men waste their money, neglect their families, break their wives' hearts, and set a bad example to their children. People better die than drink, and make brutes of themselves. Lots of money is wasted. Folks kill other folks when they are drunk, and steal, and lie, and do every bad thing. Now, my friends (I mean you pigs), turn from your evil ways, and drink no more. . . . Here is the pledge; come and sign it. Keep it all your lives, and be good men. (I mean pigs.)"

Here Jimmy smiled, but he meant what he said, and, pulling out of his pocket a piece of paper and a pencil, he jumped down to use the block as a desk, saying, as he wrote in big letters, "They shall have a pledge, and they can make a mark as people do who can't write. I'll make it short, so they can understand it, and I know they will keep it, for I shall help them."

So busy was the boy with his work that he never saw a man steal from behind the pen where he had been listening, and laughing at Jimmy's lecture, till something seemed to change the smiles to tears, for, as he peeped over the lad's shoulder, he saw how worn the little jacket was, how bruised and blistered the poor hands were with too hard work, and how he stood on one foot, because his toes were out of the old shoes.

A month's wages were in the man's pocket, and he meant to spend them in more whisky when his jug was empty. Now the money seemed all too little to make his son tidy, and he couldn't bear to think how much he had wasted on low pleasures that made a worse brute of him than the pigs.

"There!" said Jimmy, "I guess that will do. We, Tom and Jerry, do solemnly promise never to touch, taste, or handle anything that can make us drunk."

"Now for the names. Which shall mark first?"

"I will!" said the man, startling Jimmy so much that he nearly tumbled into the pen as he was climbing up. The paper fluttered down inside, and both forgot it as the boy looked up at the man, saying, half ashamed, half glad,—

"Why, father, did you hear me? I was only sort of playing."

"I am in earnest, for your lecture was a very good one; and I'm not going to be a beast any longer. Here's money for new shoes and jacket. Give me the saw. I'll do my own work now, and you go tell mother what I say."

Jimmy was about to race away, when the sight of Tom and Jerry eating up the paper made him clap his hands, exclaiming joyfully,—

"They've taken the pledge really and truly. I'm so glad!"

It was impossible to help laughing; but the man was very sober again as he said slowly, with his hand on Jimmy's shoulder,—

"You shall write another for me. I'll sign it, and keep it too, if you will help me, my good little son."

"I will, father, I will!" cried Jimmy with all his happy heart, and then ran in to carry the good news to mother.

That was his first lecture, but not his last; for he delivered many more when he was a man, because the work begun that day prospered well, and those pledges were truly kept.

L. M. Alcott on Dress

(*An Old-Fashioned Girl*, 1870)

Another thing that troubled Polly was her clothes, for, though no one said anything, she knew they were very plain; and now and then she wished that her blue and mouse colored merinos were rather more trimmed, her sashes had bigger bows, and her little ruffles more lace on them. She sighed for a locket, and, for the first time in her life, thought seriously of turning up her pretty curls and putting on a "wad." She kept these discontents to herself, however, after she had written to ask her mother if she might have her best dress altered like Fanny's, and received this reply:

"No, dear; the dress is proper and becoming as it is, and the old fashion of simplicity the best for all of us. I don't want my Polly to be loved for her clothes, but for herself; so wear the plain frocks mother took such pleasure in making for you, and let the *panniers* go. The least of us have some influence in this big world; and perhaps my little girl can do some good by showing others that a contented heart and a happy face are better ornaments than any Paris can give her. You want a locket, deary; so I send one that my mother gave me years ago. You will find father's face on one side, mine on the other; and when things trouble you, just look at your talisman, and I think the sunshine will come back again."

Of course it did, . . . that good old fashion of simplicity made the plain gowns pretty, and the grace of unconsciousness beautified their little wearer. . . .

"You are fourteen; and *we* consider ourselves young ladies at that age," continued Fanny [to Polly], surveying, with complacency, the pile of hair on the top of her head, with a fringe of fuzz round her forehead, and a wavy lock streaming down her back; likewise, her scarlet-and-black suit, with its big sash, little *pannier,* bright buttons, points, rosettes,—and, heaven knows what. There was a locket on her neck, earrings tinkling in her ears, watch and chain at her belt, and several rings on a pair of hands that would have been improved by soap and water.

. . . "My mother likes me to dress simply, and I don't mind. I shouldn't know what to do rigged up as you are. Don't you ever forget to lift your sash and fix those puffy things when you sit down?" . . .

It is a well-known fact, that dress plays a very important part in the lives of most women; and even the most sensible cannot help owning, sometimes, how much happiness they owe to a becoming gown, gracefully arranged hair, or a bonnet which brings out the best points in their faces, and puts them in a good humor. . . . It is not the finest dress which does the most execution, I fancy, but that which best interprets individual taste and character. Wise people understand this.

L. M. Alcott on Dress

(*Eight Cousins*, 1875)

"The idea of cramping a tender little waist in a stiff band of leather and steel just when it ought to be growing," said Dr. Alec, surveying the belt with great disfavor as he put the clasp forward several holes. . . .

"Nature knows how to mould a woman better than any corset-maker, . . . *have* you lost your senses that you can for a moment dream of putting a growing girl into an instrument of torture like this?" and with a sudden gesture he [Dr. Alec] plucked forth the offending corsets . . . and held them out with the expression one would wear on beholding the thumbscrews or the rack of ancient times.

"Whalebones indeed! A regular fence of them, and metal gate-posts in front. As if our own bones were not enough, if we'd give them a chance to do their duty," growled the Doctor.

2

Health and Alternative Medicine:
Homeopathy, Phrenology,
Mind Cure

Organon of the Healing Art

(Author's Preface to Sixth Edition; published as
Organon of Medicine, Philadelphia, 1922)

SAMUEL C. F. HAHNEMANN

. . . to give a general notion of the treatment of disease pursued by the old school of medicine (allopathy). . . . It assails the body with large doses of powerful medicines, . . . and by their long-continued employment it develops in the body new and often ineradicable medicinal diseases. Whenever it can, it employs . . . remedies that immediately suppress and hide the morbid symptoms by opposition . . . for a short time (palliatives), but that leave the cause of these symptoms (the disease itself) strengthened and aggravated. . . .

This non-healing art . . . has shortened the lives of ten times as many human beings as the most destructive wars, and rendered many millions of patients more diseased and wretched than they were originally. . . . Now I shall consider its exact opposite, the true healing art, discovered by me. . . . Examples are given to prove that striking cures performed in former times were always due to remedies basically homeopathic and found by the physician accidentally and contrary to the then prevailing methods of therapeutics.

As regards the latter (homeopathy) it is quite otherwise. It can easily convince every reflecting person that . . . diseases of man are . . . spirit-like (dynamic) derangements of the spirit-like power (the vital principle) that animates the human body. Homeopathy knows that a cure can only take place by the reaction of the vital force against the rightly chosen remedy that has been ingested, and that the cure will be certain and rapid in proportion to the strength with which the vital force still prevails in the patient. Hence homeopathy

. . . employs for the cure ONLY those medicines whose power for altering and deranging (dynamically) the health it knows *accurately*, and from these it selects one whose pathogenic power (its medicinal disease) is capable of removing the natural disease in question by similarity . . . and this it administers to the patient in simple form, but in rare and minute doses so small that, without occasioning pain or weakening, they just suffice to remove the natural malady . . . and the patient, even whilst he is getting better, gains in strength and thus is cured. . . .

Synopsis of Phrenology and Physiology

(1845)

L. N. FOWLER

The first principle of Phrenology is—the brain is the organ of the mind. . . .

Now all men believe in the union of mind with matter in some form, and to a certain extent. Phrenologists say, this union is with the brain. . . .

The second principle of Phrenology is—the brain is not an unit, but a compound organ, containing a plurality of organs, each one of which developes one of the special faculties. . . . these separate organs are each of them one of a congeries. . . . They occupy the same relation to each other as the mental faculties; or, the brain has its organs, as the mind has its faculties. . . .

SIZE THE MEASURE OF POWER. This is the third principle of Phrenology. It is applied to the absolute size of the brain as a whole; or to its parts as such.

. . . the province of the phrenologist is to point out the *character* or *kind* of talents and mental power. . . .

The *Vital* or *Nutritive Temperament,* imparting vital power, gives fulness and health to the body; manufactures vitality; sustains and prolongs life; and re-supplies the brain and muscles with the animal energy exhausted by their action; giving restlessness of body, and love of air and exercise. . . .

The *Muscular* or *Motive Temperament* is intimately connected with the osseous system, and gives strength, prominence to shape, with power and endurance of body and mind.

The *Mental* or *Nervous Temperament,* upon which the mind de-

41

pends for manifestation, embracing the brain and nervous system, gives clearness, activity, and penetration of mind; intensity of feeling; love of study; and highly wrought susceptibilities; also, quickness, sprightliness of mind, brilliancy of talent, general smartness, and a wide awake turn of mind.

CLASSIFICATION OF THE FACULTIES.

The first natural division of the mind is into *Intellect* and *Feeling.*— Intellect giving thought, reason, judgment, discernment, knowledge, memory, system and wit, is located in the frontal lobe of the brain, giving height, width, length, and prominence to the forehead.

The Feelings, giving impulse, executiveness, appetite, ambition, pride, will, sympathy, love, and sentiment, are located in the coronal, occipital, and basilar portions of the brain. . . .

DOMESTIC PROPENSITIES.

Amativeness.—The passion of love and attraction between the sexes as such; desire to caress and fondle. Abuse: Licentiousness and obscenity. Deficiency: Want of attention, love and regard to the opposite sex.

Philoprogenitiveness.—Parental love; regard for children, pets, and animals, and attention to their wants. Abuse: Spoiling children by caressing. Deficiency: Neglect of the young.

Adhesiveness.—Friendship; attachment; affection; desire for society, to congregate, to associate, and to entertain friends. Abuse: Too great fondness for company; indiscriminate connections. Deficiency: Neglect of friends and society. . . .

SELFISH PROPENSITIES.

Vitativeness.—Love of life; desire to exist; dread of death. Abuse: Extreme tenacity of life; over-anxious about health; too great dread of sickness. Deficiency: Recklessness as to life and health; unnecessary exposures of health, and exhaustion of vital powers.

Combativeness.—Self-protection; defence; personal courage; resistance; boldness; resolution; the let-me-alone disposition. Abuse: Pugnacity; a quick, fiery, ungovernable temperament; a fault-finding, contentious disposition. Deficiency: Want of courage and disposition to contend for rights.

Destructiveness.—Executiveness; energy; indignation; hatred; retribution; and a destroying, pain-causing, exterminating disposition. Abuse: Rage; malice; revenge; premeditated cruelty; murder. Deficiency: Extreme gentleness. . . .

Phrenology unfolds to us the true nature and elements of the mind, their adaptation to the various conditions, relations, and wants of man.

It furnishes us the data by means of which we may become acquainted with ourselves and others.

It enables us to know the true function of all the faculties of the mind, and what kind of action and exercise they need.

It lays the foundation for a correct system of education. Guided by it, the minds of children will receive their true bias, and be educated with reference to their real natural powers of mind, so as to balance and perfect the character; as well as to "train up the child in the way he should go."

It furnishes us a true definition of virtue and vice.

It gives us a true system of mental philosophy which will harmonize with a true system of moral philosophy, and both combined will set before us the whole duty and obligations of man to his fellow man and to his Maker—thus furnishing to him a system of religion harmonizing with the principles laid down in the Bible, upon which he can rely with confidence.

It explains the cause of the great versatility of character, talent, opinion, faith, and enjoyment among men.

It enables us to make proper allowances for others, and disposes us to have the right kind of charity for those who differ from us.

A correct system of *Law, Government,* and *Punishment,* can be based upon no other foundation than that of Phrenology.

Trust in the Infinite

An Address delivered at the Woman's Educational & Industrial
Union . . . December 31, 1882 (Boston, 1885)

ANNA B. NEWMAN

Through the teachings of the Bible, and of philosophers from whom
I have quoted, I have led the way to the thought that man is mind;
that the body of man, which most persons call the Real, is only an
appearance or reflection, or shadowing forth. . . . The physical nature is only the reflection or shadow of mind. . . . We shall work out
on our bodies (which, as I before stated, are only shadows or reflections of mind) the harmony, peace, and health which we desire. . . .
In other words, it is the separation in our minds of the Real and the
Unreal; calling that real which has eternal Life, and the Unreal
which has death and decay in it. . . .

Now if by this conception of God, living in the Real, diseases are
healed that physicians have pronounced incurable, is it not wise to
put aside our opinions and prejudices? . . .

Many may say, "I don't believe my thinking in that way would
ever alter any condition in my body." True, the thinking would not
do it. It is the realization of these truths. . . .

The possibilities are in your mind, but they cannot be fulfilled
until you have acquired the rules of the language, and faithfully applied them; even then it may be a great while before you can convey
the real meaning or spirit of it as it existed in the mind of the poet.

Probably many of you are familiar with the account of the condemned criminal, who, being blindfolded and laid upon a table, was
told he was to be bled to death. The surgeon made a slight incision
in the flesh, a stream of water was so arranged he could constantly

hear it drop, drop, drop. The surgeon occasionally felt his pulse, and said he was growing weaker and weaker, and alluded to the quantity of blood lost.

As a result of this experiment, the man died, with every symptom of exhaustion from loss of blood, when in reality, he had lost none.

Again the experiment was tried in Europe by physicians in a hospital, with two condemned criminals. One was told the bed in which he was placed had never been occupied by a cholera patient. The truth was that it had been, even to the clothes; while the other was told the clean bed in which he was placed had been the death-bed of a cholera patient. The man in the infected bed remained perfectly well; the other died in a few hours with cholera.

Now fear produced the disease in one case, and the man without fear resisted direct contact with the poison.

There are many well-authenticated cases where great grief or anxiety has changed a person's hair white in a few hours.

Both fear and trust are mental states. Is it a more difficult act to think one thought than another? Fear in the one case made its distorted, contracted image in mind; and body (the reflection or shadowing forth of the mind) worked it out, and death resulted.

Trust made, or rather held, its image of health, and the body remained well. Fear, either conscious or unconscious, produces all discord; while faith and trust carry us unscathed through all things. . . . Now, if fear, which is of the natural mind, is so potent, must not faith, which is of the spiritual mind, have infinitely greater power? For perfect love casteth out fear. . . .

This truth has been applied in hundreds of cases, even to the healing of cancers, which are considered fatal.

L. M. Alcott on Homeopathy

(*Eight Cousins*, 1875)

[Rose to her Uncle Alec]: "I had forgotten you were a doctor. I'm glad of it, for I do want to be well, only I hope you won't give me much medicine, for I've taken quarts already, and it does me no good."

As she spoke, Rose pointed to a little table just inside the window, on which appeared a regiment of bottles.

"Ah, ha! Now we'll see what mischief these blessed women have been at." And, making a long arm, Dr. Alec set the bottles on the wide railing before him, examined each carefully, smiled over some, frowned over others, and said, as he put down the last: "Now I'll show you the best way to take these messes." And, as quick as a flash, he sent one after another smashing down into the posy-beds below.

"But Aunt Plenty won't like it; and Aunt Myra will be angry, for she sent most of them!" cried Rose, half frightened and half pleased at such energetic measures.

"You are my patient now, and I'll take the responsibility. My way of giving physic is evidently the best, for you look better already," he said, laughing so infectiously that Rose followed suit, saying saucily,—

"If I don't like your medicines any better than those, I shall throw them into the garden, and then what will you do?"

"When I prescribe such rubbish, I'll give you leave to pitch it overboard as soon as you like."

"Lines to a Good Physician, From a Grateful Patient"

(*The Pellet. A Record of the Massachusetts Homeopathic Hospital Fair*, 1872)

L. M. ALCOTT

Faithful as a leech,
  Helpful as a blister,
Soothing as morphine
  To a nervous sister;
Strengthening as a tonic,
  Sweet as sugared pill,
Comforting as ether
  In every human ill;
Searching as quinine
  In the botheration
Called "torpid or imperfect
  Portal circulation";
Living medicine chest
  Full of doses rare;
Patience, sense and skill,
  Sympathy and care,
Courtesy and kindliness,
  Both to young and old;
Charity that shows itself
  In good deeds manifold.
Cordial as old wine
  Given health to mend;
Best of earthly physic
  Bottled in a *friend.*

Phrenological Examination of L. M. Alcott

(Manuscript, 1875)

L. M. A., AGE 43

HEAD EXAMINED NOV. 22ND 1875

Faith hope & charity very large, especially the latter. Friendship re-markable, has more friends than she wants, bears others' burdens, & lets them impose on her through her strong sympathy & generosity. *Conjugal love* very marked, capable of all things for the man she loved. A devoted wife & mother. Adores children & wins thier hearts at once. Loves praise but can go without it if her will or principle makes it seem right. Leans to the *ideal,* yet from certain motives can be very practical. A good nurse through her magnetic & sympathetic power. Has the gift of language, is dramatic & witty. Strong passions but can control them. Dual nature very marked, but the higher pre-dominates through culture & moral sentiment. Great powers of ob-servation & mimicry. A good talker but not a speaker. Intellectual faculties developed largely, but great benevolence prevents entire devotion to intellectual pursuits. Conscientiousness large, will also, & the two conflict. Great vitality & a fine constitution, yet liable to overdo as the spirit is ardent & sometimes headstrong.

A person who can row *against* the tide & like it. If she wrote a story no one could tell how it was coming out as it would be sure to take an unexpected & unusual turn. Love of nature, reads character well & has great intuitive perception, understands without study & knows things by instinct.

A remarkable head.

Poem to Her Sister Anna Pratt

(January 1, 1876; inscribed on the flyleaf of Sizer's
How to Read Character [1870])

L. M. ALCOTT

TO NAN

I remember, I remember
  A doll which once you had
A plaster head with numbered bumps
  In long clothes sweetly clad.
And how you loved the funny thing
  And bore it in your arms,
A tender mother even then
  And proud of baby's charms.

Now living idols fill you heart
  And be in your embrace;
Two yellow heads, bright eyed & fair
  Smile up in mother's face.
So here's a book to help you read
  There pates from brow to crown,
Which bumps are made by growing up
  And which by tumbling down.

Jan. 1st 1876.

49

Character Analysis of L. M. Alcott Based on a Profile Portrait

(*Phrenological Journal,* April 1881)

Miss Alcott's portrait shows her to be a woman of unusual force. The profile is strong and distinct in its markings. Nose, mouth, and chin have characteristics of energy, purpose, and resolution. She is tall and spare in frame—the Motive temperament of her father being impressed upon the bodily contours, and conspicuously influencing her mental organism. She is more powerful in thought, more earnest and thorough-going as a worker, than she is delicate and symmetrical. Her convictions are deep and controlling, giving her character for independence. Her intellectual faculties are generally active, and being strong and well disciplined, she has a much broader comprehension of the matters relating to life than the average. Few persons . . . are more steadfast in opinion than she. Firmness contributes emphasis and positiveness to her conduct, supporting the impressions or conclusions obtained through the intellect.

As a member of society, judging from the portrait, she is not known for an easy disposition to conform to fashion and custom, but rather for originality of view and practicality of motive. She believes in being true to one's impressions of truth and duty; admires spirit and zeal in those who have work to perform for themselves or the world; . . . As for formalism in Church, State, or social life she has comparatively little time or regard to give in that direction.

L. M. Alcott on Mind Cure

L. M. ALCOTT TO MAGGIE LUKENS, FEBRUARY 16, 1885

. . . I have been trying the Mind Cure, & find it very wonderful. It is the power of the mind over matter, soul over body, & those who learn it can not only heal themselves but others, & live above the small pains & worries that vex so many of us. Mrs. Anna Newman is my teacher, & I enjoy it very much, it is so simple & yet so deep.

We all believe it for it is only the old faith in God & our highest self, but the application of it to pain & care is new. Many wonderful cures I *know* of, & though I cant quite see how it is done done yet, I cannot doubt it since I see the miracles wrought & feel the power myself.

Drs laugh & people call it "humbug" as they do every new idea, but I am sure a great truth is in it, & am studying it out. . . .

L. M. ALCOTT TO MAGGIE LUKENS, MARCH 15, 1885

. . . I send you a little paper about the Mind Cure, which explains the thing as much as words can.

It is very interesting & I have had some high moments, but they dont last long, & though my mind is cheered up my body does not get over its ails as I hoped.

Mrs Newman says it takes time & long training to get the art of rising above your body & compelling it to be what it ought. I have my doubts still about the truth of *all* the good enthusiasts say, but they certainly do perform wonderful cures & I know *they* are true as I see the people.

The patient sits quietly with shut eyes, & the Dr the same, for 15 minutes in silence. Some feel nothing & others a good deal.

I feel very still, then very light, & seem floating away on a sea of rest. Once or twice I seemed to have no body, & to come back from another world. I felt as if I trod on air & was very happy & young for some hours. Yet one does no sleep nor lose consciousness, & there is nothing unpleasant about it. It is not mesmerism.

The power to go into this state of rest is what we want, & many get it. "It is," they say, "simply turning to the Source of all rest & strength &, sitting passive, let it flow into one & heal & cheer body & soul."

A very sweet doctrine if one can only *do it*. I cant yet, but try it out of interest in the new application of the old truth & religion which we all believe, that soul is greater than body, & being so should rule.

This will give you something to think of & as delicate, gentle people often grasp these things more quickly than the positive ones, you may get ahead of me in the new science. Just believe that you will be better & you will, they say. Try it.

L. M. Alcott on Mind Cure

(Journal, 1885)

January

Tried the Mind Cure with Mrs Newman. Agreeable at first. Blue clouds & sunshine in my head. Mesmerism, though Mrs N. said it was *not*. Breath short, heart fluttered, seemed to float away. Could not move. Very quiet after it. Queer times. Will try the experiment & gratefully accept any miracle that can be wrought for me.

February

My mind-cure not a success. First I am told to be "passive." So I do, say & think nothing. No effect. Then I am not "positive" enough & must not try to *understand* anything. Inconsistency & too much hurry. God & Nature cant be hustled about every ten minutes to cure a dozen different ails. Too much money made & too much delusion all round.

Mrs [Frances Hodgson] Burnett is trying it. Says it quiets her mind but does n't help her body. Too much is claimed for it.

March

Mrs N[ewman] says "you've got it!" but she deceives herself for I have lost my faith & never feel any better after a seance. . . . Miss N. made no more impression on me than a moonbeam. After 30 trials I give it up. No miracle for me. My ills are not imaginary, so are hard to cure.

"Miss Alcott on Mind-Cure"

(*The Woman's Journal*, April 18, 1885)

As many invalids have written to ask my opinion of the mind-cure, and as various false reports are going about, I will briefly give my own experience, leaving others to profit by it or to try the experiment as they choose.

Writer's cramp and an overworked brain were the ills I hoped to mitigate by the new cure, of which marvellous accounts were given me. With a very earnest desire to make a fair trial, I took about thirty treatments, finding it a very agreeable and interesting experience up to a certain point. No effect was felt except sleepiness for the first few times; then mesmeric sensations occasionally came, sunshine in the head, a sense of walking on the air, and slight trances, when it was impossible to stir for a few moments.

Much cheerful conversation, the society of an agreeable person, and the hope that "springs eternal in the human breast," made these earlier weeks very pleasant. But when no bodily pain was alleviated, and instinct warned that something was wrong, I began to question and doubt a theory which claimed to cure cancers, yet could not help a headache. I made myself as passive as a reasonable being can, hoping that since lunatics and children were helped, I too could be if I gave up trying to see, believe, or understand. But when thirty treatments left the arm no better and the head much worse, I dared lose no more time, and returned to the homeopathy and massage from which I had been lured by the hope of finding a short and easy way to undo in a month the overwork of twenty years.

This is my experience, and many others who have made the experiment tell the same story, while half the fabulous cases reported to me prove to be failures like my own when investigated.

My opinion of the matter is that, being founded on a fact which no one denies, namely, the power of mind over body, there is truth in it and help, if it is not overdone and more claimed for it than is due. Every physician has cases where the mind rules the body, and works wonders with science to lend a hand; but to ignore such help and rely only on the blind groping, self-delusion, or temporary excitement which the mind-cure brings to most is a mistake.

Mesmerism, unconsciously used, perhaps, does much; curiosity, the love of the miraculous, the hope of health, and more than all, the yearning of weary spirits for Divine support, lends this new craze its charm, and attracts the crowd of sufferers who fill the rooms and pockets of the persons who profess the healing gift.

If it be all they claim, may it prosper and grow clearer, higher and stronger, for we need all the help we can get to meet the new diseases that afflict us. If it be a delusion, as some of us believe, let those who practise it beware how they coin money out of the suffering of fellow-creatures, and blindly lessen faith in God and man by promising what they cannot perform.

L. M. ALCOTT.

3

Education: Moral, Intellectual, Physical

Record of Mr. Alcott's School

(1888; first published in 1835 as *Record of a School*)

ELIZABETH PALMER PEABODY

Mr. Alcott sat behind his desk, and the children were placed in chairs in a large arc around him; the chairs so far apart that they could not easily touch each other. He then asked each one separately what idea he or she had of the purpose of coming to school. To learn, was the first answer. To learn what? By pursuing this question, all the common exercises of the school were brought up by the children themselves; and various subjects of arts, science, and philosophy. Still Mr. Alcott intimated that this was not all; and at last some one said, "To behave well;" and in pursuing this expression into its meanings, they at last agreed that they came to learn to feel rightly, to think rightly, and to act rightly. A boy of seven years old suggested that the most important of these three was right action.

Simple as all this seems, it would hardly be believed what an evident exercise it was to the children, to be led of themselves to form and express these conceptions and few steps of reasoning. Every face was eager and interested. From right actions, the conversation naturally led into the means of bringing them out. And the necessity of feeling in earnest, of thinking clearly, and of school discipline, was talked over. . . .

On . . . occasions, he conversed with them, and, by a series of questions, led them to come to conclusions for themselves upon moral conduct in various particulars; teaching them how to examine themselves, and to discriminate their animal and spiritual natures, or their outward and inward life, and showing them how the inward molds the outward. They were deeply interested in these conversations, as they would constantly declare; although, at first, those who were oftenest revealing to themselves and others their hitherto unrecognized weaknesses and faults were so deeply mortified that it was often painful. The youngest scholars were as much interested as the oldest; and, although it was necessary to explain language to them rather more, it was found less necessary to reason on moral subjects. . . .

Mr. Alcott thinks that every book read should be an event to a child; and all his plans of teaching keep steadily in view the object of making books live, breathe, and speak; and he considers the glib reading which we hear in some schools as a preventive rather than as an aid to his purposes. He has himself no doubt as to the ultimate result, not only upon the intellectual powers, but upon the very enunciation of the words, which cannot fail to borrow energy and life from the thoughts and feelings they awaken within the soul of the reader. . . .

[Alcott said]: "I have found few books to aid me. I have been thrown on my own resources, collecting from circumstances, or creating from the ideal of my own mind, the material for the spiritual nurture of children. Of the few works that have become established favorites with my scholars, the Bible, 'Pilgrim's Progress,' 'The Fairy Queen,' Krummacher's Parables, 'The Story without an End,' Miss Edgeworth's Stories, are most attractive.

"It is from such books that I read oftenest to children; for Imagination is the soul's shaping power, and, when rightly nurtured, it clothes the spirit in the robes of truth. If there be any fact settled by the history of our race, it is that Imagination has been the leading light to mankind. What, indeed, is Genius but this faculty in its liveliest activity? And Genius has shaped the institutions of society in all past ages. We need schools not alone for the inculcation of knowledge, but for the development of Genius,—the creative attribute of Spirit. And no instruction deserves the name that does not quicken this,—its essential life,—and fit it for representation in literature, art, or philosophy."

"Pilgrim's Progress," read with many omissions and some paraphrase of the text, was for the first three months the greatest favorite in this schoool. The Bible was the next favorite. In March, the test being put, it was found that the scholars were less willing to give up readings in the Bible than any thing else. The readings in the Bible were not confined to particular seasons, but were called to meet the occasions of the moment.

The first two months were given up almost entirely to this pre-liminary discipline. Two hours and a half every day were divided between the readings and conversations on conduct, and the com-parative importance of things within and without. The government was decided and clear from the first, but was not hurried beyond the comprehension of the children; for Mr. Alcott is so thoroughly convinced that all effectual government must be self-government. . . . Besides, a teacher never should forget that the mind he is direct-ing may be on a larger scale than his own; that its sensibilities may be deeper, tenderer, wider; that its imagination may be swifter; that its intellectual power of proportioning and reasoning may be more powerful; and he should ever have the humility to feel himself at times in the place of a child, and the magnanimity to teach him how to defend himself against his own (*i.e.* the teacher's) influence. By such humility, he will also be in the best road towards that deeply felt self-reliance which is founded on sober self-estimation, although entirely removed from vanity.

When he first began to teach school, he thought no punishment was desirable, and spent much time in reasoning. But, besides that this consumed a great deal of time that might have been better spent, he was convinced, in the course of his observations, that the passions of the soul could not in all cases be met by an address to the understanding, and only were diverted, not conquered, by being reasoned with. What would excite feeling, he found must be brought to bear upon wrong feeling, when that actually existed, and to rouse sensibility when there was a deficiency.

Deeper observations of life and of human nature convinced him that the ministry of pain was God's great means of developing strength and elevation of character; and that children should early understand this, that they might accept it as a moral blessing. He, therefore, introduced punishment by name, and found that, in the-orizing on the subject with his scholars, there was a general feeling of its desirableness and necessity; and he never failed in obtaining their consent to it as a general principle. On some occasions, there was to be corporeal correction, to consist of one blow with a ferule upon the palm of the hand, more or less severe according to the age and necessities of the pupil. When this was administered, it was always to be accompanied with conversation, and given in the anteroom. . . .

One morning, when he was opening "Pilgrim's Progress" to read, he said that those who had whispered or broken any rule since they came into the school might rise to be corrected. About a dozen rose. He told them they might go into the anteroom, and stay there while he was reading. They did so. The reading was very interesting, though it had been read before; for every new reading brings new associations and peculiar conversation. Those in the anteroom could hear the occasional bursts of feeling which the reading and conversation elicited. A lady who was present went out just before the reading closed, and found those who had been sent out sitting, looking very disconsolate and perfectly quiet, though no directions had been given to them. She expressed her regret at their losing the interesting reading. Oh, yes, we know! said they; we have heard them shout. Nothing is so interesting as "Pilgrim's Progress" and the conversations, said one. We would rather have been punished any other way. . . .

Having brought the whole school to this state of feeling, Mr. Alcott introduced a new mode. He talked with them; and having again adverted to the necessity of pain, in a general point of view, and brought them to acknowledge the uses of this hurting of the body (as he always phrased it) in concentrating attention, &c, he said that he should have it administered upon his own hand for a time, instead of theirs, but that the guilty person must do it. They declared that they would never do it. They said they preferred being punished themselves. But he determined that they should not escape the pain and the shame of administering the stroke upon him, except by being themselves blameless.

. . . Mr. Alcott has secured obedience now; there is not a boy in school but what would a great deal rather be punished himself than punish him.

Reports of the School Committee, and Superintendent of the Schools, of the Town of Concord, Mass.

With a Notice of an Exhibition of the Schools, in the Town Hall, on Saturday, March 16, 1861 (Concord, 1861)

A. BRONSON ALCOTT

Does the teacher awaken thought, strengthen the mind, kindle the affections, call the conscience, the common sense, into lively and controlling activity, so promoting the love of study, the practice of the virtues; habits that shall accompany the children outwards into life? The memory is thus best cared for, the ends of study answered, the debt of teacher to parents, of parents to children, and so the State's bounty is best bestowed. . . .

Teaching is an instinct of the heart; and with young children particularly. It needs kindly sensibilities, simple feelings and sincere; love abounding. Young women are better suited to the work, and more excellent than most men. This interest is essential in all, for admirable as one's qualities may be in other respects, and surpassing her gifts, the secret touch of sympathy is the sole spring of success. The heart is the leader and prompter. No amount of learning avails without it. . . .

Recitations. I have witnessed a growing perception on the part of teachers and pupils of the true uses of books and of their place in the order of studies. The teachers have become interpreters in some sense of the text books, and the recitations are rendered more lively and profitable in consequence: information has been methodized in the mind, a greater accuracy ensured, a firmer grasp of subjects, and pleasure associated with study. The text has been taken as a thread for conversation, and a clue to the sense, the pupils being required to render this by translation or paraphrase. The method of conversation adopted by most, has put spirit and meaning into the exercises; brought teacher and classes into livelier sympathy and correspondence with one another; into intimacies more or less friendly according to the temperament and disposition of the partners. Perhaps this change is the hopefullest sign of improvement made in our schools. A child should be dealt with sympathetically and so helped to express himself gracefully and this help comes best by conversing.

Conversation. Conversation is the mind's mouth-piece, its best spokesman; the leader elect and prompter in teaching. Practiced daily it should be added to the list of school studies; an art in itself, let it be used as such and ranked as an accomplishment second to none that nature or culture can give. Certainly the best we can do is to teach ourselves and children how to talk. . . . We want living minds to quicken and inform living minds. A boy's life, a maiden's time, is too precious to be wasted in committing words to the memory from books they never learn the use of. . . .

Pilgrim's Progress. The Pilgrim's Progress stands next to the parables of the New Testament in the value of its insinuating moralities. It should be on the desk of every teacher, and in every home library throughout Christendom. It never tires; it cannot be read too frequently; it is never finished, and the thousandth perusal is as new and as charming as the first. . . .

Ancient Culture. . . . Body and mind are yokefellows and love to draw together in these life tasks and pleasures of ours. All need meat and drink, fresh air, the influence of sunshine, exercise out of doors, and a chosen task; if imposed, the more is the need of those incitements, as reliefs and relays for us in disguise. Play is wholesome. A sound mind proves itself best by keeping its body sound and swift to serve its turns; its senses keen, its limbs strong and agile for the moment. . . .

Letters and Diaries. Every child feels early the desire for communicating his emotions and thoughts, first by conversation and next by writing. Letters and diaries are his first confidants: the records of life and the stuff of its living literature. With the writing of these let composition begin. . . .

Home Influences. The school is an index to the family, the key to home influences; it is the readiest reading of the town's population. As the family, such is the school, such is the neighborhood, the institutions, the man. It is the world in little. . . .

Parents' Visits. The school stands nearest the family of all our institutions,—is indeed an extension and image of it, and claims its fostering interest and sympathy. It should enlist the parents' affection, and get some of their freshest hours. Its teachers deserve to be taken into their hearts as friends, the friends of their children, and their assistants in the work of training them in the ways of learning and virtue. . . .

Studies in the Mind. . . . The mind with its faculties and powers are the tools we use in this work of living. By these invisible implements we deal with things and affairs. Our bodies are handles for them. And the prime office of education is to put us fairly in possession and instruct us in the sleights of their uses; their bearing directly and skilfully upon life and its opportunities. . . .

Study of the Mind. With such views to guide me, I have wished to interest the more advanced classes in the several schools in the study of the mind, for which a place has not been assigned in the order of exercises, owing to the want of a suitable text-book. Believing that something might be done, meanwhile, I have ventured some conversations in some of them, taking our scale of the faculties as a thread for discussion, using the black-board for rendering our analysis the more obvious as we proceeded. It needs more time than we have at command to take soundings in these depths of the life-powers, and deliver them to the light and to the senses. But these attempts, imperfect and unsatisfactory at best, have proved beyond question how easy it is to interest the young in those studies. A sensible teacher shall get ready responses from the Sphynxes, since nothing is so charming to mind as the mind itself when interrogated aptly and to the point.

Catalogue and Circular of Dr. Dio Lewis's Family School for Young Ladies, Lexington, Mass., 1865

(Boston, 1865)

DR. DIO LEWIS

PLAN OF THE SCHOOL.

The general design of this school is to secure a symmetrical develop-ment of body, mind, and heart; to give due attention to *physical* and *social* culture, while imparting thorough instruction in Literature, Art, Science, and Morals. . . .

The absorbing purpose of Dr. Lewis in the establishment of this school was to furnish the best possible conditions for acquiring a complete *education,* in the true and broad sense of the term. These conditions can be secured only by the most watchful attention to diet, sleep, dress, ventilation, bathing, and recreation, as well as to qualifications of teachers, and methods of instruction. Such atten-tion the *head of a family* can obviously best give. Moreover, a wise, cheerful, loving home-nurture is indispensable to the most rapid and harmonious development of the entire being.

PHYSICAL CULTURE.

It is the special and earnest aim of this School to give PHYSICAL CUL-TURE a just and honorable place in its course of instruction. Ameri-can girls, especially of the higher classes, are very many of them pale, nervous, and fragile, with stooping shoulders, weak spines, and nar-row chests. Such, in studying under the ordinary and *fashionable* systems of education, greatly imperil their physical well-being, com-

66

promise their enjoyment of life, and often break down altogether in the midst of their labors. Keenly do fine and sensitive natures suffer when high hopes of usefulness, and bright anticipations of happiness, are thus blighted in the springtime of life; but such premature decay and suffering are only penalties for violating law. If the claims of the body be wholly disregarded, or too entirely subordinated to intellectual cultivation, failure and disappointment are inevitable. But let the early training of our youth be broad and symmetrical, physiological and philosophical, and even delicate girls may endure hard study, and thrive upon it. We are RESOLVED, therefore, to *insist* upon such a style of life in our School as shall give to the body strength, endurance, and grace; and help each one of our graduates to go forth with "a sound mind in a sound body."

To carry out this purpose, we shall rely upon the following means:—

I.—Regular and thorough instruction in Anatomy and Physiology, with frequent familiar lectures on practical hygiene, and constant attention to the personal regimen of pupils.

II.—The careful practice, from two to four half-hours each day, of the *New Gymnastics;* and exercises of the *Swedish Movement Cure,* in the case of any who may need special treatment.

III.—Plain and nutritious food, such as shall best conduce to the healthy growth of muscle and brain.

IV.—Fixed hours for rising and retiring, so arranged as to secure for all, regular and abundant sleep.

V.—Baths, both warm and cold.

VI.—Regular morning and evening walks, with daily rides in favorable weather; recreations in the open air; together with a great variety of in-door sports and amusements.

VII.—A physiological dress, such as shall properly protect the body without hindering its growth, deforming its beauty, or interfering with any of its vital functions.

OUR FIRST YEAR.

After many years' anxious thought and preparation, this School was opened on the first of October, 1864. As an important innovation was to be made, it was thought best to limit the number of pupils.

Thirty was announced as the maximum number. The School was full. The young ladies ranged from twelve to twenty-three years of age. The average was seventeen. The families represented in the School are among the most intelligent in New England. Intellectually and morally, our pupils were all we could ask; physically, they were much below the average.

Accustomed to teach gymnastics among those who, living at home, indulged the fashionable errors of dress, diet, sleep, bathing, &c., Dr. Lewis had never comprehended the possibilities in physical culture. Retiring at an early hour; sleeping in large, well-ventilated rooms; visiting a plain, nutritious table at proper intervals; bathing frequently under the guidance of intelligent assistants; wearing a physiological dress; and spending several hours a day in the open air,—these concomitants added far more than had been anticipated to the results of the gymnastic training. The general development may be inferred, when it is stated, that, about the upper part of the chest, the average enlargement was two and three-quarter inches. In the physical training of this school, *lean* girls increased in flesh, while the fleshy ones became thinner and more active.

We are well satisfied that the common opinion concerning excessive brain-work in our schools is an error; but that our girls, even, may double their intellectual acquisitions, provided their exercise, bathing, diet, sleep, and other physiological conditions be rightly managed.

L. M. Alcott's Pedagogical Credo

LITTLE MEN, 1871

As there is no particular plan to this story, except to describe a few scenes in the life at Plumfield [School] for the amusement of certain little persons, we will gently ramble along . . . and tell some of the pastimes of Mrs. Jo's boys. I beg leave to assure my honored readers that most of the incidents are taken from real life, and that the oddest are the truest; for no person, no matter how vivid an imagination he may have, can invent anything half so droll as the freaks and fancies that originate in the lively brains of little people.

"What a very nice school this is!" observed Nat, in a burst of admiration.

"It's an odd one," laughed Mrs. Bhaer, "but you see we don't believe in making children miserable by too many rules, and too much study." . . . "the little minds" [are cultivated with] "the tender wisdom of a modern Pythagoras—not tasking [them] with long, hard lessons, parrot-learned, but helping [them] to unfold.". . .

Boys at other schools probably learned more from books, but less of that better wisdom which makes good men. Latin, Greek, and mathematics were all very well, but in Professor Bhaer's opinion, self-knowledge, self-help, and self-control were more important. . . .

They teach us quite as much as we teach them.

AN OLD-FASHIONED GIRL, 1870

Fanny went to a fashionable school, where the young ladies were so busy with their French, German, and Italian, that there was no time for good English. . . .

Another thing that disturbed Polly was the want of exercise. . . .

At home, Polly ran and rode, coasted and skated, jumped rope and raked hay, worked in her garden and rowed her boat; so no wonder she longed for something more lively than a daily promenade with a flock of giddy girls, who tilted along in high-heeled boots, and costumes which made Polly ashamed to be seen with some of them.

EIGHT COUSINS, 1875

She went to a dame-school and learnt a few useful things well; that is better than a smattering of half a dozen so-called branches. . . .

". . . that is considered an excellent school, I find, and I dare say it would be if the benighted lady did not think it necessary to cram her pupils like Thanksgiving turkeys, instead of feeding them in a natural and wholesome way. It is the fault of most American schools, and the poor little heads will go on aching till we learn better." . . .

"You shall teach me, and when I am a woman we will set up a school where nothing but the three Rs shall be taught, and all the children live on oatmeal, and the girls have waists a yard round," said Rose, with a sudden saucy smile.

JO'S BOYS, 1886

At [Laurence College] all found something to help them, for the growing institution had not yet made its rules as fixed as the laws of the Medes and Persians, and believed so heartily in the right of all sexes, colors, creeds, and ranks to education that there was room for everyone who knocked, [including] eager girls from the West, the awkward freedman or woman from the South, or the wellborn student whose poverty made this college a possibility when other doors were barred.

[Education] is not confined to books.

L. M. Alcott on the New Gymnastics

L. M. ALCOTT TO LOUISA C. G. BOND
(SEPTEMBER 17, 1860)

... This amiable town [Concord] is convulsed just now with a Gymnastic fever which shows itself with great violence in all the schools & young societies generally. Dr. Lewis has inoculated us for the disease & "its taken finely" for every one has become a perambulating windmill with all four sails going as if a gale had set in, & the most virulent cases present the phenomena of black eyes & excoriation of the knobby parts of the frame to say nothing of sprains & breakage of "wessels" looming in the future.

The "city fathers" approve of it & the city sons & daughters intend to show that Concord has as much muscle as brain, & be ready for another Concord fight if Louis Napoleon sees fit to covet this famous land of Emerson Hawthorne Thoreau Alcott & Co. Abby & I are among the pioneers & the delicate vegetable productions clash their cymbals in private when the beef eating young ladies faint away & become superfluous dumb belle's. . . .

"The King of Clubs and the Queen of Hearts"

(First published in *The Monitor,* April 19–June 7, 1862; reprinted in
On Picket Duty, and Other Stories, Boston, 1864)

L. M. ALCOTT

Five and twenty ladies, all in a row, sat on one side of the hall, looking very much as if they felt like the little old woman who fell asleep
on the king's highway and awoke with abbreviated drapery, for they
were all arrayed in gray tunics and Turkish continuations, profusely
adorned with many-colored trimmings. Five and twenty gentlemen,
all in a row, sat on the opposite side of the hall, looking somewhat
subdued, as men are apt to do when they fancy they are in danger
of making fools of themselves. They, also, were *en* costume, for all
the dark ones had grown piratical in red shirts, the light ones nauti-
cal in blue; and a few boldly appeared in white, making up in starch
and studs what they lost in color, while all were more or less Byronic
as to collar.

On the platform appeared a pile of dumb-bells, a regiment of
clubs, and a pyramid of bean-bags, and stirring nervously among
them a foreign-looking gentleman, the new leader of a class lately
formed by Dr. Thor Turner, whose mission it was to strengthen the
world's spine, and convert it to a belief in air and exercise, by setting
it to balancing its poles and spinning merrily, while enjoying the
"Sun-cure" on a large scale. His advent formed an epoch in the history of the town; for it was a quiet old village, guiltless of bustle,
fashion, or parade, where each man stood for what he was; and,
being a sagacious set, every one's true value was pretty accurately
known. It was a neighborly town, with gossip enough to stir the social atmosphere with small gusts of interest or wonder, yet do no

harm. A sensible, free-and-easy town, for the wisest man in it wore the worst boots, and no one thought the less of his understanding; the belle of the village went shopping with a big sun-bonnet and tin pail, and no one found her beauty lessened; oddities of all sorts ambled peacefully about on their various hobbies, and no one suggested the expediency of a trip on the wooden horse upon which the chivalrous South is always eager to mount an irrepressible abolitionist. Restless people were soothed by the lullaby the river sang in its slow journey to the sea, old people found here a pleasant place to make ready to die in, young people to survey the world from, before taking their first flight, and strangers looked back upon it, as a quiet nook full of ancient legends and modern lights, which would keep its memory green when many a gayer spot was quite forgotten. Anything based upon common sense found favor with the inhabitants, and Dr. Turner's theories, being eminently so, were accepted at once and energetically carried out. A sort of heathen revival took place, for even the ministers and deacons turned Musclemen; old ladies tossed bean-bags till their caps were awry, and winter roses blossomed on their cheeks; school-children proved the worth of the old proverb, "An ounce of prevention is worth a pound of cure," by getting their backs ready before the burdens came; pale girls grew blithe and strong swinging their dumb namesakes; and jolly lads marched to and fro embracing clubs as if longevity were corked up in those wooden bottles, and they all took "modest quenchers" by the way.

August Bopp, the new leader of the class, was a German possessing but a small stock of English, though a fine gymnast; and, being also a bashful man, the appointed moment had no sooner arrived than he found his carefully prepared sentences slipping away from his memory as the ice appears to do from under unhappy souls first mounted upon skates. An awful silence reigned; Mr. Bopp glanced nervously over his shoulder at the staring rows, more appalling in their stillness than if they had risen up and hooted at him, then piling up the bags for the seventh time, he gave himself a mental shake, and, with a crimson visage, was about to launch his first "Ladees und gentlemen," when the door opened, and a small, merry-faced figure appeared, looking quite at ease in the novel dress, as, with a comprehensive nod, it marched straight across the hall to its place among the weaker vessels.

A general glance of approbation followed from the gentlemen's side, a welcoming murmur ran along the ladies', and the fifty pairs of eyes changed their focus for a moment. Taking advantage of which, Mr. Bopp righted himself, and burst out with a decided,—

"Ladees und gentlemen: the time have arrived that we shall begin. Will the gentlemen serve the ladees to a wand, each one, then spread theirselves about the hall, and follow the motions I will make as I shall count."

Five minutes of chaos, then all fell into order, and nothing was heard but the leader's voice and the stir of many bodies moving simultaneously. An uninitiated observer would have thought himself in Bedlam; for as the evening wore on, the laws of society seemed given to the winds, and humanity gone mad. Bags flew in all directions, clubs hurtled through the air, and dumb-bells played a castinet accompaniment to peals of laughter that made better music than any band.

4

Communal Society: "The Newness"

A. Bronson Alcott to Junius Alcott

(Fruitlands, Harvard [Mass.], June 18, 1843)

Dear Brother:

I begin my letter, as you see, with dating from Harvard, not Concord, from Fruitlands, the name we give to the spot we now occupy, and which we design to use for divine ends in future. The Estate is within 2 miles of the village of Harvard, and less than one mile of Still River hamlet. It contains nearly 100 acres, all arable land, easily cultivated, and finely adapted to the culture of grains, herbs, roots, and fruit. About 15 acres are in wood, of oak, maple, walnut, chestnut, some pine, and the timber is very thrifty, and quite sufficient for fuel, and building. There is already some fruit; apples, cherries and peaches, and the intervales and hillslopes offer most favorable sites for orchards. The meadows are prolific; and the uplands bring good crops of wheat, maize, and other useful crops. . . . There are many springs which descend from the uplands into the fields and meadows and pass off into the Still River which flows on the West of us into Nashua. We are within sight of the Shaker Families in Shirley; a couple of miles distant across the Stream.—We have just completed the planting and pruning. About 3 acres of corn are now nearly ready for the hoe; we have about 2 acres in potatoes; 1 in beans; and are preparing an acre or two more for barley, carrots, turnips, beans; and have commenced ploughing for winter wheat and rie [rye]. Of oats, we have an acre of spring rie about 2 acres to harvest in their seasons.—The buildings . . . a two story dwelling house, a large barn and cow-house, with a small barn in the intervale being ill-placed, unsightly, and inconvenient, we have not redeemed for our future use: we are to inhabit the first, and store our crops in the second during the present season; when they are all to be removed by the owner from the estate, unless we are determined to convert them into the new cottages which we purpose to build in the margin of the wood, as soon as we can—within the present season we hope.—For the land $1800 was paid, and we would put as much into cottages—perhaps even more. The spot deserves all that we design in the way of ornament architectural, and agricultur[al] and will reward us for any outlay of taste, industry, and love. There is a living fountain from which we may derive water for all household uses, for drink, cooking, bathing &c, and which may easily be carried to any apartment of our dwellings, and to the gardens, and pass thence into the rich peat lands near by to the river. We are planning a dam, not far from this Spring, by which we can hope to gain a head of water of two or three feet, for mechanical uses. The place is quite remote from the busy haunts and thoroughfares of trade; it lies in a sequestered dell, and is reached by private lanes on either side. We are thus protected from the invasion of the ruder secular world, and enjoy the quietude of a dignified independence. The neighbors seem thus far quite kindly disposed. . . . There is land enough to support many persons, and facilities for almost every worthy object of desire that outward advantages can offer. . . . There are now with us, beside Mr. Lane and his boy, a Mr. Larned, lately from Mr. Ripley's community [Brook Farm], Abram whom you know, (and a most efficient soul he is;) a Mr. Bower, a year since from England, and known to Mr. Lane; and a man working . . . wages on the farm. The latter, boards and lodges at a neighbors. Several other persons are expected soon. . . . We shall have as many seekers as we deserve, and laborers and love them all. . . . We are all in the most hopeful health and spirits, I am as busy as I can well be. The farm, orchard, children, library, press, public, repairs, building &c, give me abundant care: I should have added truest delight. This dell is the canvas on which I will paint a picture (Divinity prospering the design, and adding the means)—a worthy picture for mankind. My friend Lane, blessed of the like influence, shall be a not unapt coadjutor in the humane work. . . .

Your kindred brother,
A. BRONSON ALCOTT

Junius S. Alcott
Oriskany Falls
New York

Bronson Alcott's Fruitlands

(1915)

CLARA ENDICOTT SEARS

... Robert Carter, a co-editor with James Russell Lowell of a magazine called *The Pioneer* in 1843, wrote an article called "The Newness" in after years, describing Fruitlands and Brook Farm. Of the latter he says:—

"It was a delightful gathering of men and women of superior cultivation, who led a charming life for a few years, laboring in its fields and philandering in its pleasant woods. It was little too much of a picnic for serious profit, and the young men and maidens were rather unduly addicted to moonlight wanderings in the pine grove, though it is creditable to the sound moral training of New England that little or no harm came of these wanderings—at least, not to the maidens. Brook Farm, however, was not the only Community which was founded by the disciples of the 'Newness.' There was one established in 1843 on a farm called Fruitlands, in the town of Harvard, about forty miles from Boston. This was of much more ultra and grotesque character than Brook Farm. Here were gathered the men and women who based their hopes of reforming the world and of making all things new on dress and on diet. They revived the Pythagorean, the Essenian, and the Monkish notions of Asceticism with some variations and improvements peculiarly American. The head of the institution was Bronson Alcott, a very remarkable man, whose singularities of character, conduct, and opinion would alone afford sufficient topics for a long lecture. His friend Emerson defined him to be a philosopher devoted to the science of education, and declared that he had singular gifts for awakening contemplation and aspiration in simple and in cultivated persons. . . . His writings, though quaint and thoughtful, are clumsy compared with his conversation, which has been pronounced by the best judges to have been unrivalled in grace and clearness. Mr. Alcott was one of the most foremost leaders of the 'Newness.' He swung round the circle of schemes very rapidly, and after going through a great variety of phases he maintained, at the time of the foundation of 'Fruitlands,' that the evils of life were not so much social or political as personal, and that a personal reform only could eradicate them; that self-denial was the road to eternal life, and that property was an evil, and animal food of all kinds an abomination. No animal substance, neither flesh, fish, butter, cheese, eggs, nor milk, was allowed to be used at 'Fruitlands.' They were all denounced as pollution, and as tending to corrupt the body, and through that the soul. Tea and coffee, molasses and rice, were also proscribed,—the last two as foreign luxuries,—and only water was used as a beverage.

"Mr. Alcott would not allow the land to be manured, which he regarded as a base and corrupting and unjust mode of forcing nature. He made also a distinction between vegetables which aspired or grew into the air, as wheat, apples, and other fruits, and the base products which grew downwards into the earth, such as potatoes,[1] beets, radishes, and the like. These latter he would not allow to be used. The bread of the Community he himself made of unbolted flour, and sought to render it palatable by forming the loaves into the shapes of animals and other pleasant images. He was very strict, rather despotic in his rule of the Community, and some of the members have told me they were nearly starved to death there; nay, absolutely would have perished with hunger if they had not furtively gone among the surrounding farmers and begged for food.

"One of the Fruitlanders took it into his head that clothes were an impediment to spiritual growth, and that the light of day was equally pernicious. He accordingly secluded himself in his room in a state of nature during the day, and only went out at night for exercise, with a single white cotton garment reaching from his neck to his knees.

---

1. This was a mistake on Mr. Carter's part, as they ate potatoes freely.

"Samuel Larned lived one whole year on crackers, and the next year exclusively on apples. He went to Brook Farm after the collapse of the Fruitlands Community, and when that also failed he went South, married a lady who owned a number of slaves, and settled there as a Unitarian minister." . . .

The following letter on The Consociate Family Life was written to A. Brooke of Oakland, Ohio, and published in the *Herald of Freedom,* September 8, 1843:—

Our diet is strictly the pure and bloodless kind. No animal substances, neither flesh, butter, cheese, eggs, nor milk, pollute our table or corrupt our bodies, neither tea, coffee, molasses, nor rice, tempts us beyond the bounds of indigenous productions. Our sole beverage is pure fountain water. The native grains, fruits, herbs, and roots, dressed with the utmost cleanliness and regard to their purpose of edifying a healthful body, furnish the pleasantest refections and in the greatest variety requisite to the supply of the various organs. The field, the orchard, the garden, in their bounteous products of wheat, rye, barley, maize, oats, buckwheat, apples, pears, peaches, plums, cherries, currants, berries, potatoes, peas, beans, beets, carrots, melons, and other vines, yield an ample store for human nutrition, without dependence on foreign climes, or the degeneration of shipping and trade. The almost inexhaustible variety of the several stages and sorts of vegetable growth, and the several modes of preparation, are a full answer to the question which is often put by those who have never ventured into the region of a pure and chaste diet: "If you give up flesh meat, upon what then can you live?"

Our other domestic habits are in harmony with those of diet. We rise with early dawn, begin the day with cold bathing, succeeded by a music lesson, and then a chaste repast. Each one finds occupation until the meridian meal, when usually some interesting and deep-searching conversation gives rest to the body and development to the mind. Occupation, according to the season and the weather, engages us out of doors or within, until the evening meal,—when we again assemble in social communion, prolonged generally until sunset, when we resort to sweet repose for the next day's activity.

In these steps of reform we do not rely as much on scientific reasoning of physiological skill, as on the Spirit's dictates. The pure soul, by the law of its own nature, adopts a pure diet and cleanly customs; nor needs detailed instruction for daily conduct. On a revision of our proceedings it would seem, that if we were in the right course in our particular instance, the greater part of man's duty consists in leaving alone much that he is in the habit of doing. It is a fasting from the present activity, rather than an increased indulgence in it, which, with patient watchfulness tends to newness of life. "Shall I sip tea or coffee?" the inquiry may be. No; abstain from all ardent, as from alcoholic drinks. "Shall I consume pork, beef, or mutton?" Not if you value health or life. "Shall I stimulate with milk?" No. "Shall I warm my bathing water?" Not if cheerfulness is valuable. "Shall I clothe in many garments?" Not if purity is aimed at. "Shall I prolong my dark hours, consuming animal oil and losing bright daylight in the morning?" Not if a clear mind is an object. "Shall I teach my children the dogmas inflicted on myself, under the pretence that I am transmitting truth?" Nay, if you love them intrude not these between them and the Spirit of all Truth. "Shall I subjugate cattle?" "Shall I trade?" "Shall I claim property in any created thing?" "Shall I interest myself in politics?" To how many of these questions could we ask them deeply enough, could they be heard as having relation to our eternal welfare, would the response be "Abstain"? Be not so active to do, as sincere to be. Being in preference to doing, is the great aim and this comes to us rather by a resigned willingness than a wilful activity;—which is indeed a check to all divine growth. Outward abstinence is a sign of inward fulness; and the only source of true progress is inward. We may occupy ourselves actively in human improvements;—but these unless inwardly well-impelled, never attain to, but rather hinder, divine progress in man. During the utterance of this narrative it has undergone a change in its personal expression which might offend the hypercritical; but we feel assured that you will kindly accept it as unartful offering of both your friends in ceaseless aspiration.

CHARLES LANE,

A. BRONSON ALCOTT

Harvard, Mass.,
August, 1843.

L. M. Alcott's Journal, Fruitlands, 1843

Friday 4 [August]   After breakfast I washed the dishes and then had my lessons. Father and Mr. Kay and Mr. Lane went to the Shakers and did not return till evening. After my lessons I sewed till dinner. When dinner was over I had a bath, and then went to Mrs. Willards. When I came home I played till supper time, after which I read a little in Oliver Twist, and when I had thought a little I went to bed. I have spent quite a pleasant day.

Thursday 10   I rose early. After we had done breakfast I did my morning work. Father Mother Abba and Mr. Lane went to Leominster. I ironed a little and read till dinner was ready. After dinner I bathed. Lizzy William and I went blackberring. Mother and Father came home in the evening. Though it was unpleasant without I was happy within.

Sunday 28*   After breakfast I read till 9 oclock and Father read a Parable called Nathan and I liked it very well he than asked us all what faults we wanted to get rid of I said Impatience, and Mr. Lane selfwill. We had a dinner of bread and water after which I read thought and walked till supper.

September 1843

Friday 1   I had my lessons as usual and Mr. Lane made a piece of poetry about Pestalossi I will put in

---

*Inconsistencies in recording day of the week and date of the month are doubtless to be attributed to young Alcott's carelessness.

TO PESTALOSSI

On Pestalossis sacred brow
The modest chesnut wreath
Green yesterday but fadeing now
And pasing as a breath.

September 1st   I rose at five and had my bath. I love cold water!
Then we had our singing-lesson with Mr. Lane. After breakfast I
washed dishes, and ran on the hill till nine, and had some
thoughts,—it was so beautiful up there. Did my lessons,—wrote and
spelt and did sums; and Mr. Lane read a story, "The Judicious
Father." How a rich girl told a poor girl not to look over the fence
at the flowers, and was cross to her because she was unhappy. The
father heard her do it, and made the girls change clothes. The poor
one was glad to do it, and he told her to keep them. But the rich
one was very sad; for she had to wear the old ones a week, and after
that she was good to shabby girls. I liked it very much, and I shall
be kind to poor people.

Father asked us what was God's noblest work. Anna said *men*,
but I said *babies*. Men are often bad; babies never are. We had a long
talk, and I felt better after it, and *cleared up*.

We had bread and fruit for dinner. I read and walked and played
till supper-time. We sung in the evening. As I went to bed the moon
came up very brightly and looked at me. I felt sad because I have
been cross to-day, and did not mind Mother. I cried, and then I felt
better, and said that piece from Mrs. Sigourney, "I must not tease
my mother." I get to sleep saying poetry—I know a great deal.

Thursday, 14th   Mr. Parker Pillsbury came, and we talked about
the poor slaves. I had a music lesson with Miss P. [Ann Page]. I
hate her, she is so fussy. I ran in the wind and played be a horse,
and had a lovely time in the woods with Anna and Lizzie. We were
fairies, and made gowns and paper wings. I "flied" the highest of
all. In the evening they talked about travelling. I thought about
Father going to England, and said this piece of poetry I found in
Byron's poems:—

"When I left thy shores, O Naxos,
  Not a tear in sorrow fell;
Not a sigh or faltered accent
  Told my bosom's struggling swell."

It rained when I went to bed and made a pretty noise on the roof.

Sunday, 24th Father and Mr. Lane have gone to N.H. to preach. It was very lovely. . . . Anna and I got supper. In the eve I read "Vicar of Wakefield." I was cross to-day, and I cried when I went to bed. I made good resolutions, and felt better in my heart. If I only *kept* all I make, I should be the best girl in the world. But I don't, and so am very bad.

October 8th When I woke up, the first thought I got was, "It's Mother's birthday: I must be very good." I ran and wished her a happy birthday, and gave her my kiss. After breakfast we gave her our presents. I had a moss cross and a piece of poetry for her.

We did not have any school, and played in the woods and got red leaves. In the evening we danced and sung, and I read a story about "Contentment." I wish I was rich, I was good, and we were all a happy family this day.

Thursday, 12th After lessons I ironed. We all went to the barn and husked corn. It was good fun. We worked till eight o'clock and had lamps. Mr. Russell came. Mother and Lizzie are going to Boston. I shall be very lonely without dear little Betty, and no one will be as good to me as mother. I read in Plutarch. I made a verse about sunset:—

"Softly doth the sun descend
  To his couch behind the hill.
Then, oh, then, I love to sit
  On mossy banks beside the rill."

Anna thought it was very fine; but I didn't like it very well.

Friday, Nov. 2nd Anna and I did the work. In the evening Mr. Lane asked us, "What is man?" These were our answers: A human being;

an animal with a mind; a creature; a body; a soul and a mind. After a long talk we went to bed very tired.

Tuesday, 20th I rose at five, and after breakfast washed the dishes, and then helped mother work. Miss P. is gone, and Anna in Boston with Cousin Louisa. I took care of Abba (May) in the afternoon. In the evening I made some pretty things for my dolly. Father and Mr. L. had a talk, and father asked us if *we* saw any reason for us to separate. Mother wanted to, she is so tired. I like it, but not the school part or Mr. L.

Eleven years old. Thursday, 29th It was Father's and my birthday. We had some nice presents. We played in the snow before school. Mother read "Rosamond" when we sewed. Father asked us in the eve what fault troubled us most. I said my bad temper.

I told mother I liked to have her write in my book. She said she would put in more, and she wrote this to help me:—

"Dear Louy,—Your handwriting improves very fast. Take pains and do not be in a hurry. I like to have you make observations about our conversations and your own thoughts. It helps you to express them and to understand your little self. Remember, dear girl, that a diary should be an epitome of your life. May it be a record of pure thought and good actions, then you will indeed be the precious child of your loving mother."

December 10th I did my lessons, and walked in the afternoon. Father read to us in dear Pilgrim's Progress. Mr. L. was in Boston and we were glad. In the eve father and mother and Anna and I had a long talk. I was very unhappy, and we all cried. Anna and I cried in bed, and I prayed God to keep us all together.

"Transcendental Wild Oats"

(The Independent, December 18, 1873)

L. M. ALCOTT

On the first day of June, 184–, a large wagon, drawn by a small horse and containing a motley load, went lumbering over certain New England hills, with the pleasing accompaniments of wind, rain, and hail. A serene man with a serene child upon his knee was driving, or rather being driven, for the small horse had it all his own way. A brown boy with a William Penn style of countenance sat beside him, firmly embracing a bust of Socrates. Behind them was an energetic-looking woman, with a benevolent brow, satirical mouth, and eyes brimful of hope and courage. A baby reposed upon her lap, a mirror leaned against her knee, and a basket of provisions danced about at her feet, as she struggled with a large, unruly umbrella. Two blue-eyed little girls, with hands full of childish treasures, sat under one old shawl, chatting happily together.

In front of this lively party stalked a tall, sharp-featured man, in a long blue cloak; and a fourth small girl trudged along beside him through the mud as if she rather enjoyed it.

The wind whistled over the bleak hills; the rain fell in a despondent drizzle, and twilight began to fall. But the calm man gazed as tranquilly into the fog as if he beheld a radiant bow of promise spanning the gray sky. The cheery woman tried to cover every one but herself with the big umbrella. The brown boy pillowed his head on the bald pate of Socrates and slumbered peacefully. The little girls

NOTE: For Abel Lamb, read Bronson Alcott; for Timon Lion, read Charles Lane; for Hope Lamb, read Mrs. Alcott; for Jane Gage, read Ann Page.

sang lullabies to their dolls in soft, maternal murmurs. The sharp-nosed pedestrian marched steadily on, with the blue cloak streaming out behind him like a banner; and the lively infant splashed through the puddles with a duck-like satisfaction pleasant to behold.

Thus these modern pilgrims journeyed hopefully out of the old world, to found a new one in the wilderness.

The editors of *The Transcendental Tripod* had received from Messrs. Lion & Lamb (two of the aforesaid pilgrims) a communication from which the following statement is an extract:

"We have made arrangements with the proprietor of an estate of about a hundred acres which liberates this tract from human ownership. Here we shall prosecute our effort to initiate a Family in harmony with the primitive instincts of man.

"Ordinary secular farming is not our object. Fruit, grain, pulse, herbs, flax, and other vegetable products, receiving assiduous attention, will afford ample manual occupation, and chaste supplies for the bodily needs. It is intended to adorn the pastures with orchards, and to supersede the labor of cattle by the spade and the pruning-knife.

"Consecrated to human freedom, the land awaits the sober culture of devoted men. Beginning with small pecuniary means, this enterprise must be rooted in a reliance on the succors of an ever-bounteous Providence, whose vital affinities being secured by this union with uncorrupted field and unworldly persons, the cares and injuries of a life of gain are avoided.

"The inner nature of each member of the Family is at no time neglected. Our plan contemplates all such disciplines, cultures, and habits as evidently conduce to the purifying of the inmates.

"Pledged to the spirit alone, the founders anticipate no hasty or numerous addition to their numbers. The kingdom of peace is entered only through the gates of self-denial; and felicity is the test and the reward of loyalty to the unswerving law of Love."

This prospective Eden at present consisted of an old red farmhouse, a dilapidated barn, many acres of meadow-land, and a grove. Ten ancient apple trees were all the "chaste supply" which the place offered as yet; but, in the firm belief that plenteous orchards were soon to be evoked from their inner consciousness, these sanguine founders had christened their domain Fruitlands.

Here Timon Lion intended to found a colony of Latter Day Saints, who, under his patriarchal sway, should regenerate the world and glorify his name for ever. Here Abel Lamb, with the devoutest faith in the high ideal which was to him a living truth, desired to plant a Paradise, where Beauty, Virtue, Justice, and Love might live happily together, without the possibility of a serpent entering in. And here his wife, unconverted but faithful to the end, hoped, after many wanderings over the face of the earth, to find rest for herself and a home for her children.

"There is our new abode," announced the enthusiast, smiling with a satisfaction quite undamped by the drops dripping from his hat-brim, as they turned at length into a cart-path that wound along a steep hillside into a barren-looking valley.

"A little difficult of access," observed his practical wife, as she endeavored to keep her various household gods from going overboard with every lurch of the laden ark.

"Like all good things. But those who earnestly desire and patiently seek will soon find us," placidly responded the philosopher from the mud, through which he was now endeavoring to pilot the much-enduring horse.

"Truth lies at the bottom of a well, Sister Hope," said Brother Timon, pausing to detach his small comrade from a gate, whereon she was perched for a clearer gaze into futurity.

"That's the reason we so seldom get at it, I suppose," replied Mrs. Hope, making a vain clutch at the mirror, which a sudden jolt sent flying out of her hands.

"We want no false reflections here," said Timon, with a grim smile, as he crunched the fragments under foot in his onward march.

Sister Hope held her peace, and looked wistfully through the mist at her promised home. The old red house with a hospitable glimmer at its windows cheered her eyes; and, considering the weather, was a fitter refuge than the sylvan bowers some of the more ardent souls might have preferred.

The newcomers were welcomed by one of the elect precious—a

regenerate farmer, whose idea of reform consisted chiefly in wearing white cotten raiment and shoes of untanned leather. This costume, with a snowy beard, gave him a venerable, and at the same time a somewhat bridal appearance.

The goods and chattels of the Society not having arrived, the weary family reposed before the fire on blocks of wood, while Brother Moses White regaled them with roasted potatoes, brown bread and water, in two plates, a tin pan, and one mug—his table service being limited. But, having cast the forms and vanities of a depraved world behind them, the elders welcomed hardship with the enthusiasm of new pioneers, and the children heartily enjoyed this foretaste of what they believed was to be a sort of perpetual picnic.

During the progress of this frugal meal, two more brothers appeared. One a dark, melancholy man, clad in homespun, whose peculiar mission was to turn his name hind part before and use as few words as possible. The other was a bland, bearded Englishman, who expected to be saved by eating uncooked food and going without clothes. He had not yet adopted the primitive costume, however; but contented himself with meditatively chewing dry beans out of a basket.

"Every meal should be a sacrament, and the vessels used beautiful and symbolical," observed Brother Lamb, mildly, righting the tin pan slipping about on his knees. "I priced a silver service when in town, but it was too costly; so I got some graceful cups and vases of Britannia ware."

"Hardest things in the world to keep bright. Will whiting be allowed in the community?" inquired Sister Hope, with a housewife's interest in labor-saving institutions.

"Such trivial questions will be discussed at a more fitting time," answered Brother Timon, sharply, as he burnt his fingers with a very hot potato. "Neither sugar, molasses, milk, butter, cheese, nor flesh are to be used among us, for nothing is to be admitted which has caused wrong or death to man or beast."

"Our garments are to be linen till we learn to raise our own cotton or some substitute for woollen fabrics," added Brother Abel, blissfully basking in an imaginary future as warm and brilliant as the generous fire before him.

"Haou abaout shoes?" asked Brother Moses, surveying his own with interest.

"We must yield that point till we can manufacture an innocent substitute for leather. Bark, wood, or some durable fabric will be invented in time. Meanwhile, those who desire to carry out our idea to the fullest extent can go barefooted," said Lion, who liked extreme measures.

"I never will, nor let my girls," murmured rebellious Sister Hope, under her breath.

"Haou do you cattle'ate to treat the ten-acre lot? Ef things ain't 'tended to right smart, we shan't hev no crops," observed the practical patriarch in cotton.

"We shall spade it," replied Abel, in such perfect good faith that Moses said no more, though he indulged in a shake of the head as he glanced at hands that had held nothing heavier than a pen for years. He was a paternal old soul and regarded the younger men as promising boys on a new sort of lark.

"What shall we do for lamps, if we cannot use any animal substance? I do hope light of some sort is to be thrown upon the enterprise," said Mrs. Lamb, with anxiety, for in those days kerosene and camphene were not, and gas unknown in the wilderness.

"We shall go without till we have discovered some vegetable oil or wax to serve us," replied Brother Timon, in a decided tone, which caused Sister Hope to resolve that her private lamp should be always trimmed, if not burning.

"Each member is to perform the work for which experience, strength, and taste best fit him," continued Dictator Lion. "Thus drudgery and disorder will be avoided and harmony prevail. We shall arise at dawn, begin the day by bathing, followed by music, and then a chaste repast of fruit and bread. Each one finds congenial occupation till the meridian meal; when some deep-searching conversation gives rest to the body and development to the mind. Healthful labor again engages us till the last meal, when we assemble in social communion, prolonged till sunset, when we retire to sweet repose, ready for the next day's activity."

"What part of the work do you incline to yourself?" asked Sister Hope, with a humorous glimmer in her keen eyes.

"I shall wait till it is made clear to me. Being in preference to doing is the great aim, and this comes to us rather by a resigned willingness than a willful activity, which is a check to all divine growth," responded Brother Timon.

"I thought so." And Mrs. Lamb sighed audibly, for during the year he had spent in her family Brother Timon had so faithfully carried out his idea of "being, not doing," that she had found his "divine growth" both an expensive and unsatisfactory process.

Here her husband struck into the conversation, his face shining with the light and joy of the splendid dreams and high ideals hovering before him.

"In these steps of reform, we do not rely so much on scientific reasoning or physiological skill as on the spirit's dictates. The greater part of man's duty consists in leaving alone much that he now does. Shall I stimulate with tea, coffee, or wine? No. Shall I consume flesh? Not if I value health. Shall I subjugate cattle? Shall I claim property in any created thing? Shall I trade? Shall I adopt a form of religion? Shall I interest myself in politics? To how many of these questions— could we ask them deeply enough and could they be heard as having relation to our eternal welfare—would the response be 'Abstain'?"

A mild snore seemed to echo the last word of Abel's rhapsody, for Brother Moses had succumbed to mundane slumber and sat nodding like a massive ghost. Forest Absalom, the silent man, and John Pease, the English member, now departed to the barn; and Mrs. Lamb led her flock to a temporary fold, leaving the founders of the "Consociate Family" to build castles in the air till the fire went out and the symposium ended in smoke.

The furniture arrived next day, and was soon bestowed; for the principal property of the community consisted in books. To this rare library was devoted the best room in the house, and the few busts and pictures that still survived many flittings were added to beautify the sanctuary, for here the family was to meet for amusement, instruction, and worship.

Any housewife can imagine the emotions of Sister Hope, when she took possession of a large, dilapidated kitchen, containing an old stove and the peculiar stores out of which food was to be evolved for her little family of eleven. Cakes of maple sugar, dried peas and beans, barley and hominy, meal of all sorts, potatoes, and dried fruit. No milk, butter, cheese, tea, or meat, appeared. Even salt was considered a useless luxury and spice entirely forbidden by these lovers of Spartan simplicity. A ten years' experience of vegetarian vagaries had been good training for this new freak, and her sense of the ludicrous supported her through many trying scenes.

Unleavened bread, porridge, and water for breakfast; bread, vegetables, and water for dinner; bread, fruit, and water for supper was the bill of fare ordained by the elders. No teapot profaned that sacred stove, no gory steak cried aloud for vengeance from her chaste gridiron; and only a brave woman's taste, time, and temper were sacrificed on that domestic altar.

The vexed question of light was settled by buying a quantity of bayberry wax for candles; and, on discovering that no one knew how to make them, pine knots were introduced, to be used when absolutely necessary. Being summer, the evenings were not long, and the weary fraternity found it no great hardship to retire with the birds. The inner light was sufficient for most of them. But Mrs. Lamb rebelled. Evening was the only time she had to herself, and while the tired feet rested the skilful hands mended torn frocks and little stockings, or anxious heart forgot its burden in a book.

So "mother's lamp" burned steadily, while the philosophers built a new heaven and earth by moonlight; and through all the metaphysical mists and philanthropic pyrotechnics of that period Sister Hope played her own little game of "throwing light," and none but the moths were the worse for it.

Such farming probably was never seen before since Adam delved. The band of brothers began by spading garden and field; but a few days of it lessened their ardor amazingly. Blistered hands and aching backs suggested the expediency of permitting the use of cattle till the workers were better fitted for noble toil by a summer of the new life.

Brother Moses brought a yoke of oxen from his farm—at least, the philosophers thought so till it was discovered that one of the animals was a cow; and Moses confessed that he "must be let down easy, for he couldn't live on garden sarse entirely."

Great was Dictator Lion's indignation at this lapse from virtue. But time pressed, the work must be done; so the meek cow was permitted to wear the yoke and the recreant brother continued to enjoy forbidden draughts in the barn, which dark proceeding caused the children to regard him as one set apart for destruction.

The sowing was equally peculiar, for, owing to some mistake, the three brethren, who devoted themselves to this graceful task, found when about half through the job that each had been sowing a different sort of grain in the same field; a mistake which caused much perplexity, as it could not be remedied; but, after a long consultation and a good deal of laughter, it was decided to say nothing and see what would come of it.

The garden was planted with a generous supply of useful roots and herbs; but, as manure was not allowed to profane the virgin soil, few of these vegetable treasures ever came up. Purslane reigned supreme, and the disappointed planters ate it philosophically, deciding that Nature knew what was best for them, and would generously supply their needs, if they could only learn to digest her "sallets" and wild roots.

The orchard was laid out, a little grafting done, new trees and vines set, regardless of the unfit season and entire ignorance of the husbandmen, who honestly believed that in the autumn they would reap a bounteous harvest.

Slowly things got into order, and rapidly rumors of the new experiment went abroad, causing many strange spirits to flock thither, for in those days communities were the fashion and transcendentalism raged wildly. Some came to look on and laugh, some to be supported in poetic idleness, a few to believe sincerely and work heartily. Each member was allowed to mount his favorite hobby and ride it to his heart's content. Very queer were some of the riders, and very rampant some of the hobbies.

One youth, believing that language was of little consequence if the spirit was only right, startled newcomers by blandly greeting them with "good morning, damn you," and other remarks of an equally mixed order. A second irrepressible being held that all the emotions of the soul should be freely expressed, and illustrated his theory by antics that would have sent him to a lunatic asylum, if, as an unregenerate wag said, he had not already been in one. When his spirit soared, he climbed trees and shouted; when doubt assailed him, he lay upon the floor and groaned lamentably. At joyful periods, he raced, leaped, and sang; when sad, he wept aloud; and when a great thought burst upon him in the watches of the night, he crowed like a jocund cockerel, to the great delight of the children and the great annoyance of the elders. One musical brother fiddled whenever so moved, sang sentimentally to the four little girls, and put a music-box on the wall when he hoed corn.

Brother Pease ground away at his uncooked food, or browsed over the farm on sorrel, mint, green fruit, and new vegetables. Occasionally he took his walks abroad, airily attired in an unbleached cotton *poncho,* which was the nearest approach to the primeval costume he was allowed to indulge in. At midsummer he retired to the wilderness, to try his plan where the woodchucks were without prejudices and huckleberry bushes were hospitably full. A sunstroke unfortunately spoilt his plan, and he returned to semi-civilization a sadder and wiser man.

Forest Absalom preserved his Pythagorean silence, cultivated his fine dark locks, and worked like a beaver, setting an excellent example of brotherly love, justice, and fidelity by his upright life. He it was who helped overworked Sister Hope with her heavy washes, kneaded the endless succession of batches of bread, watched over the children, and did the many tasks left undone by the brethren, who were so busy discussing and defining great duties that they forgot to perform the small ones.

Moses White placidly plodded about, "chorin' raound," as he called it, looking like an old-time patriarch, with his silver hair and flowing beard, and saving the community from many a mishap by his thrift and Yankee shrewdness.

Brother Lion domineered over the whole concern; for, having put the most money into the speculation, he was resolved to make it pay—as if anything founded on an ideal basis could be expected to do so by any but enthusiasts.

Abel Lamb simply revelled in the Newness, firmly believing that his dream was to be beautifully realized, and in time not only little Fruitlands, but the whole earth, be turned into a Happy Valley. He worked with every muscle of his body, for *he* was in deadly earnest. He taught with his whole head and heart; planned and sacrificed, preached and prophesied, with a soul full of the purest aspirations, most unselfish purposes, and desires for a life devoted to God and man, too high and tender to bear the rough usage of this world.

It was a little remarkable that only one woman ever joined this community. Mrs. Lamb merely followed wheresoever her husband led—"as ballast for his balloon," as she said, in her bright way.

Miss Jane Gage was a stout lady of mature years, sentimental, amiable, and lazy. She wrote verses copiously, and had vague yearnings and graspings after the unknown, which led her to believe herself fitted for a higher sphere than any she had yet adorned.

Having been a teacher, she was set to instructing the children in the common branches. Each adult member took a turn at the infants; and, as each taught in his own way, the result was a chronic state of chaos in the minds of these much-afflicted innocents.

Sleep, food, and poetic musings were the desires of dear Jane's life, and she shirked all duties as clogs upon her spirit's wings. Any thought of lending a hand with the domestic drudgery never occurred to her; and when to the question, "Are there any beasts of burden on the place?" Mrs. Lamb answered, with a face that told its own tale, "Only one woman!" the buxom Jane took no shame to herself, but laughed at the joke, and let the stout-hearted sister tug on alone.

Unfortunately, the poor lady hankered after the fleshpots, and endeavored to stay herself with private sips of milk, crackers, and cheese, and on one dire occasion she partook of fish at a neighbor's table.

One of the children reported this sad lapse from virtue, and poor Jane was publicly reprimanded by Timon.

"I only took a little bit of the tail," sobbed the penitent poetess.

"Yes, but the whole fish had to be tortured and slain that you might tempt your carnal appetite with that one taste of the tail. Know ye not, consumers of flesh meat, that ye are nourishing the wolf and tiger in your bosoms?"

At this awful question and the peal of laughter which arose from some of the younger brethren, tickled by the ludicrous contrast be-

tween the stout sinner, the stern judge, and the naughty satisfaction of
the young detective, poor Jane fled from the room to pack her trunk,
and return to a world where fishes' tails were not forbidden fruit.

Transcendental wild oats were sown broadcast that year, and the
fame thereof has not yet ceased in the land; for, futile as this crop
seemed to outsiders, it bore an invisible harvest, worth much to those
who planted in earnest. As none of the members of this particular
community have ever recounted their experiences before, a few of
them may not be amiss, since the interest in these attempts has never
died out and Fruitlands was the most ideal of all these castles in Spain.

A new dress was invented, since cotton, silk, and wool were forbidden as the product of slave-labor, worm-slaughter, and sheep-robbery.
Tunics and trowsers of brown linen were the only wear. The women's
skirts were longer, and their straw hat-brims wider than the men's,
and this was the only difference. Some persecution lent a charm to the
costume, and the long-haired, linen-clad reformers quite enjoyed the
mild martyrdom they endured when they left home.

Money was abjured, as the root of all evil. The produce of the
land was to supply most of their wants, or be exchanged for the few
things they could not grow. This idea had its inconveniences; but
self-denial was the fashion, and it was surprising how many things
one can do without. When they desired to travel, they walked, if
possible, begged the loan of a vehicle, or boldly entered car or coach,
and, stating their principles to the officials, took the consequences.
Usually their dress, their earnest frankness, and gentle resolution
won them a passage; but now and then they met with hard usage,
and had the satisfaction of suffering for their principles.

On one of these penniless pilgrimages they took passage on a
boat, and, when fare was demanded, artlessly offered to talk, instead
of pay. As the boat was well under way and they actually had not a
cent, there was no help for it. So Brothers Lion and Lamb held forth
to the assembled passengers in their most eloquent style. There must
have been something effective in this conversation, for the listeners
were moved to take up a contribution for these inspired lunatics,
who preached peace on earth and goodwill to man so earnestly, with
empty pockets. A goodly sum was collected; but when the captain
presented it the reformers proved that they were consistent even in

their madness, for not a penny would they accept, saying, with a look at the group about them, whose indifference or contempt had changed to interest and respect, "You see how well we get on without money;" and so went serenely on their way, with their linen blouses flapping airily in the cold October wind.

They preached vegetarianism everywhere and resisted all temptations of the flesh, contentedly eating apples and bread at well-spread tables, and much afflicting hospitable hostesses by denouncing their food and taking away their appetites, discussing the "horrors of shambles," the "incorporation of the brute in man," and "on elegant abstinence the sign of a pure soul." But, when the perplexed or offended ladies asked what they should eat, they got in reply a bill of fare consisting of "bowls of sunrise for breakfast," "solar seeds of the sphere," "dishes from Plutarch's chaste table," and other viands equally hard to find in any modern market.

Reform conventions of all sorts were haunted by these brethren, who said many wise things and did many foolish ones. Unfortunately, these wanderings interfered with their harvest at home; but the rule was to do what the spirit moved, so they left their crops to Providence and went a-reaping in wider and, let us hope, more fruitful fields than their own.

Luckily, the earthly providence who watched over Abel Lamb was at hand to glean the scanty crop yielded by the "uncorrupted land," which, "consecrated to human freedom," had received "the sober culture of devout men."

About the time the grain was ready to house, some call of the Oversoul wafted all the men away. An easterly storm was coming up and the yellow stacks were sure to be ruined. Then Sister Hope gathered her forces. Three little girls, one boy (Timon's son), and herself, harnessed to clothes-baskets and Russia-linen sheets, were the only teams she could command; but with these poor appliances the indomitable woman got in the grain and saved food for her young, with the instinct and energy of a mother-bird with a brood of hungry nestlings to feed.

This attempt at regeneration had its tragic as well as comic side, though the world only saw the former.

With the first frosts, the butterflies, who had sunned themselves in the new light through the summer, took flight, leaving the few bees to see what honey they had stored for winter use. Precious little appeared beyond the satisfaction of a few months of holy living.

At first it seemed as if a chance to try holy dying also was to be offered them. Timon, much disgusted with the failure of the scheme, decided to retire to the Shakers, who seemed to be the only successful community going.

"What is to become of us?" asked Mrs. Hope, for Abel was heart-broken at the bursting of his lovely bubble.

"You can stay here, if you like, till a tenant is found. No more wood must be cut, however, and no more corn ground. All I have must be sold to pay the debts of the concern, as the responsibility is mine," was the cheering reply.

"Who is to pay us for what we have lost? I gave all I had—furniture, time, strength, six months of my children's lives—and all are wasted. Abel gave himself body and soul, and is almost wrecked by hard work and disappointment. Are we to have no return for this, but leave to starve and freeze in an old house, with winter at hand, no money, and hardly a friend left, for this wild scheme has alienated nearly all we had. You talk much about justice. Let us have a little, since there is nothing else left."

But the woman's appeal met with no reply but the old one: "It was an experiment. We all risked something, and must bear our losses as we can."

With this cold comfort, Timon departed with his son, and was absorbed into the Shaker brotherhood, where he soon found that the order of things was reversed, and it was all work and no play.

Then the tragedy began for the forsaken little family. Desolation and despair fell upon Abel. As his wife said, his new beliefs had alienated many friends. Some thought him mad, some unprincipled. Even the most kindly thought him a visionary, whom it was useless to help till he took more practical views of life. All stood aloof, saying: "Let him work out his own ideas, and see what they are worth."

He had tried, but it was a failure. The world was not ready for Utopia yet, and those who attempted to found it only got laughed at for their pains. In other days, men could sell all and give to the poor, lead lives devoted to holiness and high thought, and, after the persecution was over, find themselves honored as saints or martyrs. But in modern times these things are out of fashion. To live for one's principles, at all costs, is a dangerous speculation; and the failure of an ideal, no matter how humane and noble, is harder for the world to forgive and forget than bank robbery or the grand swindles of corrupt politicians.

Deep waters now for Abel, and for a time there seemed no passage through. Strength and spirits were exhausted by hard work and too much thought. Courage failed when, looking about for help, he saw no sympathizing face, no hand outstretched to help him, no voice to say cheerily:

"We all make mistakes, and it takes many experiences to shape a life. Try again, and let us help you."

Every door was closed, every eye averted, every heart cold, and no way open whereby he might earn bread for his children. His principles would not permit him to do many things that others did; and in the few fields where conscience would allow him to work, who would employ a man who had flown in the face of society, as he had done?

Then this dreamer, whose dream was the life of his life, resolved to carry out his idea to the bitter end. There seemed no place for him here—no work, no friend. To go begging conditions was as ignoble as to go begging money. Better perish of want than sell one's soul for the sustenance of his body. Silently he lay down upon his bed, turned his face to the wall, and waited with pathetic patience for death to cut the knot which he could not untie. Days and nights went by, and neither food nor water passed his lips. Soul and body were dumbly struggling together, and no word of complaint betrayed what either suffered.

His wife, when tears and prayers were unavailing, sat down to wait the end with a mysterious awe and submission; for in this entire resignation of all things there was an eloquent significance to her who knew him as no other human being did.

"Leave all to God," was his belief; and in this crisis the loving soul clung to his faith, sure that the All-wise Father would not desert this child who tried to live so near to Him. Gathering her children about her, she waited the issue of the tragedy that was being enacted in that solitary room, while the first snow fell outside, untrodden by the footprints of a single friend.

But the strong angels who sustain and teach perplexed and troubled souls came and went, leaving no trace without, but working miracles within. For, when all other sentiments had faded into dimness, all other hopes died utterly; when the bitterness of death was nearly over, when body was past any pang of hunger or thirst, and soul stood ready to depart, the love that outlives all else refused to die. Head had bowed to defeat, hand had grown weary with too heavy tasks, but heart could not grow cold to those who lived in its tender depths, even when death touched it.

"My faithful wife, my little girls—they have not forsaken me, they are mine by ties that none can break. What right have I to leave them alone? What right to escape from the burden and the sorrow I have helped to bring? This duty remains to me, and I must do it manfully. For their sakes, the world will forgive me in time; for their sakes, God will sustain me now."

Too feeble to rise, Abel groped for the food that always lay within his reach, and in the darkness and solitude of that memorable night ate and drank what was to him the bread and wine of a new communion, a new dedication of heart and life to the duties that were left him when the dreams fled.

In the early dawn, when that sad wife crept fearfully to see what change had come to the patient face on the pillow, she found it smiling at her, saw a wasted hand outstretched to her, and heard a feeble voice cry bravely, "Hope!"

What passed in that little room is not to be recorded except in the hearts of those who suffered and endured much for love's sake. Enough for us to know that soon the wan shadow of a man came forth, leaning on the arm that never failed him, to be welcomed and cherished by the children, who never forgot the experiences of that time.

"Hope" was the watchword now; and, while the last logs blazed on the hearth, the last bread and apples covered the table, the new commander, with recovered courage, said to her husband:

"Leave all to God—and me. He has done his part; now I will do mine."

"But we have no money, dear."

"Yes, we have. I sold all we could spare, and have enough to take us away from this snowbank."

"Where can we go?"

"I have engaged four rooms at our good neighbor, Lovejoy's. There we can live cheaply till spring. Then for new plans and a home of our own, please God."

"But, Hope, your little store won't last long, and we have no friends."

"I can sew and you can chop wood. Lovejoy offers you the same pay as he gives his other men; my old friend, Mrs. Truman, will send me all the work I want; and my blessed brother stands by us to the end. Cheer up, dear heart, for while there is work and love in the world we shall not suffer."

"And while I have my good angel Hope, I shall not despair, even if I wait another thirty years before I step beyond the circle of the sacred little world in which I still have a place to fill."

So one bleak December day, with their few possessions piled on an ox-sled, the rosy children perched atop, and the parents trudging arm in arm behind, the exiles left their Eden and faced the world again.

"Ah, me! my happy dream. How much I leave behind that never can be mine again," said Abel, looking back at the lost Paradise, lying white and chill in its shroud of snow.

"Yes, dear; but how much we bring away," answered brave-hearted Hope, glancing from husband to children.

"Poor Fruitlands! The name was as great a failure as the rest!" continued Abel, with a sigh, as a frost-bitten apple fell from a leafless bough at his feet.

But the sigh changed to a smile as his wife added, in a half-tender, half-satirical tone:

"Don't you think Apple Slump would be a better name for it, dear?"

5

Antislavery and Abolition

Americans, Freemen

(1854)

VIGILANCE COMMITTEE [RE: ANTHONY BURNS]

It has been established out of the mouths of many witnesses that the poor prisoner [Anthony Burns] now in the SLAVE PEN! Court Square! Is NOT the Slave of the KIDNAPPER SUTTLE!! Commissioner Loring will doubtless so decide to-day! The spirit of our laws and the heart within us declare that a man must not be tried twice for the same offense!

BUT will the victim then be set free? BELIEVE IT NOT; UNTIL YOU SEE IT!! The Fugitive Slave BILL was framed with a devilish *cunning* to meet such cases. It allows that a man may be tried again. It allows that if one Commissioner refuses to deliver up a man claimed as a slave to his pursuer he may be taken before a second Commissioner, and a third until some one is found base enough to do the work!!

HALLETT IS AT WORK! Burns will be seized again!—have another MOCK TRIAL, and be forced away. SEE YOU TO IT!! Let there be no armed resistance, but let the whole people turn out and line the streets and look upon the shame and disgrace of Boston, and then go away and take measures to elect men to office who will better guard the honor of the State and Capitol

Per order of the

VIGILANCE COMMITTEE

Boston, May 31, 1854

NOTE: The fugitive slave Anthony Burns was arrested in Boston on May 24, 1854, and on June 2 was returned to his owner. Alcott was among those who witnessed the rendition, and Anthony Burns would provide her with a literary source.

George and Mary Mauzy of Harpers Ferry to James and Eugenia Burton

(1859)

TO EUGENIA BURTON, ENFIELD, ENGLAND
October 17, 1859
Monday afternoon
4 o'clock

Oh my dear friend such a day as this. Heaven forbid that I should ever witness such another.

Last night a band of ruffians took possession of the town, took the keys of the armory and made Captive a great many of our Citizens. I cannot write the particulars for I am too Nervous. For such a sight as I have just beheld. Our men chased them in the river just below here and I saw them shot down like dogs. I saw one poor wrech [sic] rise above the water and some one strike him with a club he sank again and in a moment they dragged him out a Corpse. I do not know yet how many are shot but I shall never forget the sight. They just marched two wreches their Arms bound fast up to the jail. My dear husband shouldered his rifle and went to join our men May god protect him. Even while I write I hear the guns in the distance I heard they were fighting down the street.

I cannot write any more I must wait and see what the end will be.

—M. E. MAUZY

TO EUGENIA BURTON, ENFIELD, ENGLAND
October 18, 1859

This has been one of the saddest days that Harper's Ferry ever experienced. This morning, when the armorers went to the shops to go to work, lo and behold, the shops had been taken possession of by a set of abolitionists and the doors were guarded by Negroes with rifles.

—GEORGE MAUZY

TO MR. & MRS. JAMES H. BURTON

December 3, 1859

My dear Children:

Well the great agony is over. "Old Osawatomie Brown" was executed yesterday at noon—his wife came here the day before, & paid him a short visit, after which she returned here under an escort, where she and her company remained until the body came down from Charlestown, in the evening, after which she took charge of it and went home.

This has been one of the most remarkable circumstances that ever occurred in this country, this old fanatic made no confession whatever, nor concession that he was wrong, but contended that he was right in everything he done, that he done great service to God, would not let a minister of any denomination come near or say anything to him, but what else could be expected from him, or anyone else who are imbued with "Freeloveism, Socialism, Spiritualism," and all the other isms that were ever devised by man or devil.

There is an immense concourse of military at Charlestown, not less than 2000 men are quartered there, the Courthouse, all the churches & all the Lawyers offices are occupied. We have upwards of 300 regulars & 75 or 80 Montgomery Guards. These men were all sent here by the Sec. of War & Gov. Wise to prevent a rescue of Brown & his party by northern infidels and fanatics: of which they boasted loudly, but their courage must have oozed out of their finger ends, as none made their appearance. We are keeping nightly watch, all are vigilant, partys of 10 men out every night, quite a number of incendiary fires have taken place in this vicinity & County, such as grain stacks, barns & other out-buildings.

—GEORGE MAUZY

John Brown's Speech before the Court

(1859)

I have, may it please the Court, a few words to say.

In the first place, I deny everything but what I have all along admitted: of a design on my part to free slaves. . . .

Had I interfered in the matter which I admit, and which I admit has been fairly proved . . . had I so interfered in behalf of the rich, the powerful, the intelligent, or the so-called great . . . and suffered and sacrificed, what I have in this interference, it would have been all right. Every man in this Court would have deemed it an act worthy of reward rather than punishment.

I see a book kissed which I suppose to be the Bible, or at least the New Testament, which teaches me that all things whatsoever I would that men should do unto me, I should do even so to them. It teaches me further to remember them that are in bonds as bound with them. I endeavored to act up to that instruction. I say that I am yet too young to understand that God is any respecter of persons. I believe that to have interfered as I have done, as I have always freely admitted I have done in behalf of His despised poor, I did no wrong, but right. Now if it is deemed necessary that I should forfeit my life for the furtherance of the ends of justice and mingle my blood further with the blood of my children and with the blood of millions in this slave country whose rights are disregarded by wicked, cruel and unjust enactments, I say, let it be done.

[Before his death sentence was carried out on December 2, 1859, Brown issued a prophetic warning:]

I wish to say furthermore, that you had better—all you people at the South—prepare yourselves for a settlement of that question that must come up for settlement sooner than you are prepared for it. The sooner you are prepared the better. You may dispose of me very easily; I am nearly disposed of now; but this question is still to be settled—this negro question I mean—the end of that is not yet.

Civil War Nurse: The Diary and Letters of Hannah Ropes

(Edited by John R. Brumgardt, Knoxville, 1980)

HANNAH ROPES

HANNAH ROPES TO A FORMER PATIENT

Union Hospital
Georgetown, D.C.
December 29, 1862

My Dear boy,

I was very glad to hear of your safe arrival home, for it seemed a long while since you left the hospital.

Your roommates have nearly all changed since you left. Only Frocin and Lee remain. The former will be sent to St. Elizabeth's Hospital for the fitting [of] his leg.

Since the last battle, the house is full of very bad cases; some 20 amputated limbs, to say nothing of other wounds. Your room has two with one leg, and one with only a right arm. Upstairs one man has only a part of one hand left, and that is now useless from the wound. So you will understand that we have our hearts and hands full. We have one Rebel in the ballroom with an amputated leg, and we take just as good care of him as of anyone. Everything goes on nicely. The Christmas celebration was a great success, and the men had plenty of poultry and oysters. The weather is as warm as June and the air cheering. I am glad to know you're among friends; and you must not feel at all as though you shall not get entirely well. I never expected that you could go back to the camp. Army life demands just what you have lost, ability to travel. But you are young;

recuperative power is inherent in the young, and you may be even a stronger man for the idle life you are obliged to live just now. Years from now, you will be surprised to look back and feel how full the items of today filled your thoughts and clouded your hopes. Believe me, no cause for real grief or sadness lies outside of ourselves. What we *are,* no circumstances can take from us.

HANNAH ROPES TO HER SON EDWARD

Union Hospital
January 9, 1863

My Dear Neddie,

I have been sick, or you should have heard from me sooner. Only think how near you are to me. Why don't you get a furlough for a few days and come see me? I think you better write to Miss Stevenson. I don't agree with Alice about the state pay, and I wish if it can be, to be secured to me, or you, [or] Alice, as you please. I am doing my last work now. The tax upon us women who work for the love of it is tremendous when we have a new arrival of wounded, as on the 17th ult. Miss Kendall has had to go to bed, one knee refusing to walk or bend. . . .

Miss Alcott and I worked together over four dying men and saved all but one, the finest of the four, but whether [due to] our sympathy for the poor fellows, or we took cold, I know not, but we both have pneumonia and have suffered terribly. She is a splendid young woman. Can I send you a bundle? Miss Stevenson gave me a beautiful shirt for you. I should like to send you a pound of tea or some of Kate Whitner's gingerbread if I knew you would get it—can't you come over? . . .

Your loving marm,
H.A.R.

HANNAH ROPES'S LAST LETTER,
TO HER DAUGHTER ALICE

January 11, 1863

Dear Alice,

Have not had time to write before, the house has been very sick and we nurses have fairly run down. Miss Kendall is in her room, to rest for a day or two. She would not give up till her knee fairly refused to bend at all! And so she is in bed, much to my relief. Miss Alcott, of Concord, began to cough as soon as she got here. The whole house of patients, some in with lung irritations, [were similarly afflicted] and with her at first I thought it was purely sympathetic. Today she has "orders" from me not to leave her room and has a mustard plaster all over her chest. As for myself, the "head surgeon" placed me "under arrest" the day before New Years and visits me twice a day. Mrs. Boyce wanted me to go home with her, but he would not yield. I have a promise that by next Sabbath I may go. My last patient, who was so crazy, whose hand I held so long till he fell asleep, upset me. It was, the Doctor said, "the drop too much." But the boy is doing well, and came and took tea by my bed last night. My experience of sickness has been (not romantic) what so many cows have died of within the last year—pneumonia. I am glad the poor things died, but very glad I did not, for your sake, my precious little girl.

I have had the devoted attention of the whole house, and all the surgeons say even if I can't do anything at all, I *must stay* or the house will go down! Stuff. I think the rest will do me good. Mercy! What do the women at home know of work? *We never* stopped till the whole house were pronounced doing well. Now we can afford to lie by for a week. There is no patient who don't know [that] at any hour of night or day they could send to me—that makes them feel comfortable and so they recuperate. . . . Our weather is soft as June, and clear sunshine; still, not as healthy as the summer. I don't like the condition of anything and shall go home as soon as your *warm* time comes.

Your mother*

---

*Like Alcott, Hannah Ropes contracted "typhoid pneumonia," and in Ropes's case the illness proved fatal. She died in January 1863.

Some Recollections of the Antislavery Conflict

(Boston, 1869)

SAMUEL JOSEPH MAY

To complete, *by moral and religious means and instruments,* the great work which the American revolutionists commenced; to do what they left undone; to exterminate from our land the worst form of oppression, the tremendous sin of slavery, was the sole purpose of the enterprise of the Abolitionists, commenced in January, 1831. In this great work Mr. Garrison has been the leader from the beginning. Of him, therefore, I shall have the most to say. But of many other noble men and women I shall have occasion to make most grateful mention. . . .

On my return from Europe, early in November, 1859, the steamer stopped as usual at Halifax. There we first received the tidings of John Brown's raid, and the failure of his enterprise. I felt at once that it was "the beginning of the end" of our conflict with slavery. There were several Southern gentlemen and ladies among our fellow-passengers, and Northern sympathizers with them, as well as others of opposite opinions. During our short passage from Halifax to Boston there was evidently a deep excitement in many bosoms. Occasionally words of bitter execration escaped the lips of one and another of the proslavery party. But there was no dispute or general conversation upon the subject. The event, of which we had just heard, was a portent of too much magnitude to be hastily estimated, and the consequences thereof flippantly foretold.

NOTE: These recollections were recorded by the reformer and Unitarian clergyman Samuel Joseph May, who served as an antislavery agent and also happened to be Alcott's beloved uncle.

On my arrival in Boston, and the next day in Syracuse, I found the public in a state of high excitement; and for two or three months the case of John Brown was the subject of continual debate in private circles as well as public meetings. The murmurs and threats that came daily from the South, intimated plainly enough that the slaveholding oligarchy were preparing for something harsher than a war of words. They were gathering themselves to rule or ruin our Republic. Under the imbecile administration of Mr. Buchanan, the Secretary of War, John B. Floyd, could do as he saw fit in his department. It was observed that the arms and ammunition of the nation, with the greater part of the small army needed in times of peace, were removed and disposed of in such places as would make them most available to the Southerners, if the emergency for which they were preparing should come. They awaited only the issue of the next presidential contest. The first ten months of the year 1860 were given to that contest. All the strength of the two political parties was put in requisition, drawn out, and fully tested and compared. And when victory crowned the friends of freedom and human rights,—when the election of Mr. Lincoln was proclaimed,—then came forth from the South the fierce cry of disunion, and the standard of a new Confederacy was set up. It is not my intention to enter upon the period of our Civil War. These Recollections will close with occurrences before the fall of Fort Sumter. . . .

For more than thirty years the Abolitionists had been endeavoring to rouse the people to exterminate slavery by moral, ecclesiastical, and political instrumentalities, urging them to their duty by every religious consideration, and by reiterating the solemn admonition of Thomas Jefferson, that "If they would not liberate the enslaved in the land by the generous energies of their own minds and hearts, the slaves would be liberated by the awful processes of civil and servile war." But the counsels of the Abolitionists were spurned, their sentiments and purposes were shamelessly misrepresented, their characters traduced, their property destroyed, their persons maltreated. And lo! our country, favored of Heaven above all others, was given up to fratricidal, parricidal, and for a while we feared it would be suicidal war.

God be praised! the threatened dissolution of our Union was

averted. But discord still reigns in the land. Our country is not surely saved. It was right that our Federal Government should be forbearing in their treatment of the Southern Rebels, because the people of the North had been, to so great an extent, their partners in the enslavement of our fellow-men, that it would have ill become us to have punished them condignly. But our Government has been guilty of great injustice to the colored population of the South, who were all loyal throughout the war. These should not have been left as they have been, in a great measure, at the mercy of their former masters. Homes and adequate portions of the land (they so long had cultivated without compensation) ought to have been secured to every family of the Freedmen, and some provision for their education should have been made. With these and the elective franchise conferred upon them, the Freedmen might safely have been left to maintain themselves in their new condition, and work themselves out of the evils that were enforced upon them by their long enslavement.

May the sad experience of the past prompt and impel our nation, before it be too late, to do all for the colored population of our country, South and North, that righteousness demands at our hands.

L. M. Alcott on Slavery and Antislavery

L. M. ALCOTT, "WITH A ROSE, THAT BLOOMED ON THE DAY OF JOHN BROWN'S MARTYRDOM"

The Liberator, January 20, 1860

In the long silence of the night,
  Nature's benignant power
Woke aspirations for the light
  Within the folded flower. . . .

Then blossomed forth a grander flower,
  In the wilderness of wrong,
Untouched by Slavery's bitter frost,
  A soul devout and strong. . . .

No monument of quarried stone,
  No eloquence of speech,
Can grave the lessons on the land
  His martyrdom will teach. . . .

L. M. ALCOTT TO ANNA ALCOTT

(November [1856])

My Deares Nan,
  . . . Monday—Wrote all the morning copying "Ruth." After dinner I went out to see the Sumner demonstration, & having missed Lu Willis went to Beacon St. & there saw one of my idols very finely.

NOTE: Alcott championed not only the fugitive slave Anthony Burns but the stance of Senator Charles Sumner, who had been caned on the Senate floor by Representative Preston S. Brooks of South Carolina.

Eight hundred gentlemen on hors[e]back escorted him & formed a line up Beacon St. through which he rode smiling & bowing, he looked pale but otherwise as usual. I suppose you have seen an account of it, but it was better to see the real thing, so I shall tell you about it. The only time Sumner rose along the route was when he passed the Orphan Asylum & saw all the little blue aproned girls waving their hands to him. I thought it was very sweet in him to do that honor to the fatherless & motherless children. A little child was carried out to give him a great bouquet, which he took & kissed the baby bearer. The streets were lined with wreaths, flags, & loving people to welcome the good man back, & as he rode up Beacon St. where many of the houses were shut I thought of the time when Daniel Webster a great, gloomy, disappointed man passed that way & found them all open, with flowers & handsome women & shouting gentlemen to comfort him as he went by, & tho I was only a "love lorn" governess I waved my cotton handkerchief like a meek banner to *my* hero with honorable wounds on his head & love of little children in his heart. Hurra!!

I could not hear the speeches at the State House so I tore down Hancock St. & got a place opposite his house. I saw him go in, & soon after the cheers of the horsemen & crowd brought him smiling to the window, he only bowed, but when the leader of the cavelcade cried out "Three cheers for the *mother* of Charles Sumner!" he stepped back & soon appeared leading an old lady who nodded, waved her hand, put down the curtain, & then with a few dozzen more cheers the crowd dispersed.

I was so excited I pitched about like a mad woman, shouted, waved, hung onto fences, rushed thro crowds, & swarmed about in a state [of] rapterous insanity till it was all over & then I went home hoarse & worn out.

I was very sorry I didnt go with Lu for she was with Parker's party & had a fine time. They were in Tremont St. almost alone (for everyone scrambled across the Common to see the State House fun) & when Sumner passed, Parker burst out with three great cheers all by himself, the ladies clapped, & Sumner laughed like a boy as he waved his hat to his best friend. Was'nt it funny & like Parker? . . .

L. M. ALCOTT TO ANNA ALCOTT PRATT

Sunday Morn, [27? May] 1860.

. . . Thursday we set our house in order, and at two the rush began.
It had gone abroad that Mr. M. and Mrs. Captain Brown were to
adorn the scene, so many people coolly came who were not invited,
and who had no business here. People sewed and jabbered till Mrs.
Brown, with Watson Brown's widow and baby came, then a levee
took place. The two pale women sat silent and serene through the
clatter, and the bright-eyed, handsome baby received the homage of
the multitude like a little king, bearing the kisses and praises with
the utmost dignity. He is named Frederick Watson Brown, after his
murdered uncle and father, and is a fair, heroic-looking baby, with
a fine head, and serious eyes that look about him as if saying, "I am
a Brown! Are these friends or enemies?" I wanted to cry once at the
little scene the unconscious baby made. Some one caught and kissed
him rudely, he didn't cry, but looked troubled, and rolled his great
eyes anxiously about for some familiar face to reassure him with its
smile. His mother was not there, but though many hands were
stretched to him, he turned to Grandma Bridge, and putting out his
little arms to her as if she was a refuge, laughed and crowed as he
had not done before when she danced him on her knee. The old
lady looked delighted, and Freddy patted the kind face, and cooed
like a lawful descendant of that pair of ancient turtle doves.

When he was safe back in the study, playing alone at his mother's
feet, C. [probably Anna's sister-in-law Caroline Pratt] and I went
and worshipped in our own way at the shrine of John Brown's
grandson, kissing him as if he were a little saint, and feeling highly
honored when he sucked our fingers, or walked on us with his honest little red shoes, much the worse for wear.

Well, the baby fascinated me so that I forgot a raging headache
and forty gabbling women all in full cloak. Mrs. Brown, Sen., is a
tall, stout woman, plain, but with a strong, good face, and a natural
dignity that showed she was something better than a "lady," though
she *did* drink out of her saucer and used the plainest speech.

The younger woman had such a patient, heart-broken face, it was
a whole Harper's Ferry tragedy in a look. When we got your letter,

Mother and I ran into the study to read it. Mother read aloud, for there were only C., A. [probably Abby May Alcott], I, and Mrs. Brown, Jr., in the room. As she read the words that were a poem in their simplicity and happiness, the poor young widow sat with tears rolling down her face, for I suppose it brought back her own wedding-day, not two years ago, and all the while she cried the baby laughed and crowed at her feet as if there was no trouble in the world.

The preparations had been made for twenty at the utmost, so when forty souls with the usual complement of bodies appeared, we grew desperate, and our neat little supper turned into a regular "tea fight." A., C., B., and I rushed like comets to and fro trying to fill the multitude that would eat fast and drink like sponges. I filled a big plate with all I could lay my hands on, and with two cups of tea, strong enough for a dozen, charged upon Mr. E. and Uncle S., telling them to eat, drink, and be merry, for a famine was at hand. They cuddled into a corner, and then, feeling that my mission was accomplished, I let the hungry *wait* and the thirsty *moan* for tea while I picked out and helped the regular Antislavery set.

We got through it, but it was an awful hour; and Mother wandered in her mind, utterly lost in a grove of teapots; while B. prevaded the neighborhood demanding hot water, and we girls sowed cake broadcast through the land.

When the plates were empty and the teapots dry, people wiped their mouths and confessed at last that they had done. A conversation followed, in which Grandpa B. [John Bridge, John Pratt's grandfather] and E. P. P. [Elizabeth Palmer Peabody] held forth, and Uncle and Father mildly upset the world, and made a new one in which every one desired to take a place. Dr. B[artlett]., Mr. B., T[horeau?]., etc., appeared, and the rattle continued till nine, when some Solomon suggested that the Alcotts must be tired, and every one departed but C. and S. We had a polka by Mother and Uncle, the lancers by C. and B., and an *étude* by S., after which scrabblings of feast appeared, and we "drained the dregs of every cup," all cakes and pies we gobbled up, etc.; then peace fell upon us, and our remains were interred decently.

L. M. ALCOTT TO EDWARD J. BARTLETT
AND GARTH WILKINSON JAMES

Concord Dec 4th 1862

Dear Old Boys

At the last minute we hear of the box about to be sent for your jollification & comfort, & though in a great fume to do no end of things for you, we have only time to fly up garret & fill a pair of bags with nuts & apples & all good wishes for our private & particular boys. Ned! your sisters say you like apple sauce so I beg you'll have as many messes as you like out of the apples that grew in the old trees by the straw-berry bed where Wilkie stood one day with his hands in his pockets while we fed him with berries till he was moved to remark with a luxurious condescenion, "hell this is rather a nice way of eating fruit is'nt it?". You dont have time for that sort of amusement now, do you Sergeant?

The nuts are a sort of edible contraband, black, hard to take care of & not much in them in the end, but if the President cracks nuts as thoroughly as I suspect you will these, we shall soon have you home again to play whist & sing, "Pop, pop, pop"! We miss you very much and are dreadfully reduced in the gentleman line, school parties are an aggravation to the female mind. Lint Picks languish, Game parties are a myth & forlorn damsels ride & walk with never a peg-top or muffiny cap to bare them company.

Something must be done soon for even the Town School is deprived of its Shepard & Stone & a venerable Fulsom with a pair of daughters takes the place of the departed Dominies.

Abby & I play beau to the best of our ability but its not the genuine thing you see, & we sadly bewail the loss of the "Slashers & Crashers" who have deserted us for "the tented field" the only sort of desertion they will ever be guilty of as every one knows.

Now boys, if you intend to be smashed in any way just put it off till I get to Washington to mend you up, for I have enlisted & am only waiting for my commission to appear as a nurse at the "Armory" Something Hospital so be sure you are taken there, if your arms or legs fly away, some day (which the Lord forbid!) & we will have good times in spite of breakages & come out jolly under creditable circumstances like Dickens "Mark Taply."

Is there anything the old ladies can send you in the next box? Do give it a name if there is & let us help feed, clothe or assure the Defenders of the Faith if we cant take a hand in the fighting.

Father, mother, Abby and the great grey city cat all send regards & love & would rejoice to receive a line from either of you, if any odd minutes occur when home letters are done or duty dont call.

Bless your buttons & long may you wave is the parting sentiment of your

affectionate old friend

L. M. ALCOTT.

L. M. ALCOTT TO ALFRED WHITMAN

Concord Sept [1863]

My dear old Dolphus.

Carrie sent me word the other day that you felt badly because we none of us wrote, & you wanted to hear. Of course all the times I'd planned to write you & didn't, immediately rose up before me & in a great state of remorse I rush at my pen here at six oclock in the morning & scribble a line to my beloved Tetterby.

My only excuse is I've been to Washington a nursin in the army, got typhoid fever & came bundling home to rave, & ramp, & get my head shaved & almost retire into the tombs in consequence, not to mention picking up again, & appearing before the eyes of my grateful country in a wig & no particular flesh on my bones, also the writing of Hospital Sketches & when folks said put em in a book, doing the same & being drove wild with proof, & printers, & such matters, besides keeping house, seeing company, adoring my nephew, & furnishing literary gems for sundry papers—Thus you see I have not been idle though I've seemed to neglect my old boy.

How do you come on? What are you doing? & when are you coming East to be clutched at & kissed by all the "girls you left behind you?" Annie says Carrie showed her a fine picture of your father & self & writes me that Dolphus has gone & growed up in the most appalling manner. Now I wish to know what you mean by that? I'm not changed a bit, barring the wig, & I dont wish my boys to be men folks in this rapid manner. Wilkie James has gone & been made Adjutant in the 54th, got smashed at Fort Wagner & blossomed into a hero, his brother, a sixteen year older, has put on a Lieutenant's shoulder straps & pranced off with the 55th. Julian Hawthorne has set up a manly whisker & got into college, so all my boys are gone & I'm a love lorn Sophy.

Among my hospital fellows was a jolly little Sergeant who had lost his right arm at Fredericksburg—he learned to write with his left hand & sends me the funniest letters you ever saw. He has got a false arm, shouldered his rifle & is going back to his regiment for "another dig at those thundering rebs" as he says.

Dont you feel inclined to give them a slap? or are [you] helping in the peaceful & perhaps more sensible ways?

Carrie probably has told all the news about her family so I will mention what my own is up to just now, though we go on pretty much as usual. Father writes & sees to his schools, mother sings "Glory Hallelujah" over the papers & makes berry pies, Ab has been at Clark's Island with a party of young people from New York & Concord. Rowing, dancing, sailing, flirting & singing are the amusements in which they spend their shining hours. She says she is as brown as a berry & as plump as a partridge, so her trip has done her good. Annie & her John brood over the infant Freddy who is the one perfect & divine brat in the world though his nose turns straight up & he has n't half a dozen hairs on his head.

I live in my inkstand scribble, scribble from morning till night & am more peckish than ever if disturbed.

There we are & I hope you recognize the picture.

Our Concord company is to return tonight & the town is in as wild a state of excitement as it is possible for such a dozy old place to be without dying of brain fever. Flags are flapping every where, wreaths & "Welcome home" are stuck on every stickable place & our drum corps, consisting of eight small boys with eight large drums, keep a continual rub-a-dubbing.

Now my son drop me a line & send one of your new "picters" that I may behold your manly charms. I have no photographs now & must wait till my plumage is renewed when I will return the favor as I believe that is ettiquette.

Bless your buttons & "adoo".

Yours Ever   SOPHY TETTERBY.

L. M. ALCOTT TO MR. RAND

Boston Oct. 23rd [n.y.]

My Dear Mr Rand.

I send you herewith the few facts concerning my short hospital experience, a fuller account of which, if needed, can be found in the little book Hospital Sketches, made from letters at the time.

I enlisted in Dec. 1862, & was nurse in the Union Hotel temporary hospital at Georgetown. Mrs Ropes of Boston was Matron, & I took Miss Hannah Stevenson's place with Miss Julia Kendal. There were about four hundred patients, as many who were too feeble to go on to Washington were left there to die.

We had men from Fredericksburg & Antietam, as well as some from various skirmishes.

The hospital was badly managed, & all the nurses were ill from bad air & food & overwork, as ten women were all we had.

Mrs Ropes died during my stay, & I narrowly escaped with my life after a fever which left me an invalid for the rest of my days. But I never have regretted that brief yet costly experience, "(only two months,)" for all that is best & bravest in the hearts of man & woman comes out in times like those, & the courage, loyalty, fortitude and selfsacrifice I saw & learned to love & admire in both Northern & Southern soldiers can never be forgotten.

I have no picture taken about the time but the likeness of the shadow 3 mos after my illness. The one I send is not very good but it is the nearest to the war-times of any I have.

I wish I had a fuller record to offer, but as one who gladly gave her dearest possession, health, to serve the good cause I may perhaps deserve a humble place among the women who did what they could.

Thanking you for the honor,

I am yrs truly

L. M. ALCOTT.

L. M. ALCOTT TO THOMAS WENTWORTH HIGGINSON

Concord Nov 12th [1863]

My Dear Mr Higginson.

To receive a letter with Beaufort at the beginning & "Higginson" at the end was both a surprise & honor for which I thank you, as for the commendation & the criticism.

I knew that my contraband did not talk as he should, for even in Washington I had no time to study the genuine dialect, & when the story was written here I had no one to tell me how it should be.

The hospital ship & the "row of dusky faces" were taken from a letter of Mrs Gage's, describing her visit & interview with the Wagner heroes in Hilton Head harbor. Perhaps she was mistaken, in the locality, women often are inaccurate when their sympathies are at work.

I should like of all things to go South & help the blacks as I am no longer allowed to nurse the whites. The former seemed the greater work, & would be most interesting to me. I offered to go as a teacher on one of the Islands but Mr Philbrey objected because I had no natural protector to go with me, so I was obliged to give that up.

Fields spoke of engaging some letters for his Magazine if I did go, & I was much disappointed as I was willing to rough it anywhere for a time both for the sake of the help it would be to me in many ways, & the hope that I might be of use to others.

Dont you want a cook, nurse, or somewhat venerable "Child" for your regiment? I am willing to enlist in any capacity for the blood of old Col May asserts itself in his granddaughter in these martial times & she is very anxious to be busied in some more loyal labor than sitting quietly at home spinning fictions when such fine facts are waiting for all of us to profit by & celebrate.

Father & mother desire to be remembered.

Very Truly Yours
L. M. ALCOTT.

Hospital Sketches

(Boston, 1863)

BY LOUISA MAY ALCOTT

CHAPTER III. A DAY.

"They've come! they've come! hurry up, ladies—you're wanted."

"Who have come? the rebels?"

This sudden summons in the gray dawn was somewhat startling to a three days' nurse like myself, and, as the thundering knock came at our door, I sprang up in my bed, prepared

> "To gird my woman's form,
> And on the ramparts die,"

if necessary; but my room-mate took it more coolly, and, as she began a rapid toilet, answered my bewildered question,—

"Bless you, no child; it's the wounded from Fredericksburg; forty ambulances are at the door, and we shall have our hands full in fifteen minutes."

"What shall we have to do?"

"Wash, dress, feed, warm and nurse them for the next three months, I dare say. Eighty beds are ready, and we were getting impatient for the men to come. Now you will begin to see hospital life in earnest, for you won't probably find time to sit down all day, and may think yourself fortunate if you get to bed by midnight. Come to me in the ball-room when you are ready; the worst cases are always carried there, and I shall need your help."

So saying, the energetic little woman twirled her hair into a button at the back of her head, in a "cleared for action" sort of style, and vanished, wrestling her way into a feminine kind of pea-jacket as she went.

I am free to confess that I had a realizing sense of the fact that my hospital bed was not a bed of roses just then, or the prospect before me one of unmingled rapture. My three days' experiences had begun with a death, and, owing to the defalcation of another nurse, a somewhat abrupt plunge into the superintendence of a ward containing forty beds, where I spent my shining hours washing faces, serving rations, giving medicine, and sitting in a very hard chair, with pneumonia on one side, diptheria on the other, two ty-phoids opposite, and a dozen dilapidated patriots, hopping, lying, and lounging about, all staring more or less at the new "nuss," who suffered untold agonies, but concealed them under as matronly an aspect as a spinster could assume, and blundered through her trying labors with a Spartan firmness, which I hope they appreciated, but am afraid they didn't. Having a taste for "ghastliness," I had rather longed for the wounded to arrive, for rheumatism wasn't heroic, neither was liver complaint, or measles; even fever had lost its charms since "bathing burning brows" had been used up in ro-mances, real and ideal. But when I peeped into the dusky street lined with what I at first had innocently called market carts, now unload-ing their sad freight at our door, I recalled sundry reminiscences I had heard from nurses of longer standing, my ardor experienced a sudden chill, and I indulged in a most unpatriotic wish that I was safe at home again, with a quiet day before me, and no necessity for being hustled up, as if I were a hen and had only to hop off my roost, give my plumage a peck, and be ready for action. A second bang at the door sent this recreant desire to the right about, as a little woolly head popped in, and Joey, (a six years' old contraband,) announced—

"Miss Blank is jes' wild fer ye, and says fly round right away. They's comin' in, I tell yer, heaps on 'em—one was took out dead, and I see him,—hi! warn't he a goner!"

With which cheerful intelligence the imp scuttled away, singing like a blackbird, and I followed, feeling that Richard was *not* himself again, and wouldn't be for a long time to come.

The first thing I met was a regiment of the vilest odors that ever assaulted the human nose, and took it by storm. Cologne, with its seven and seventy evil savors, was a posybed to it; and the worst of this affliction was, every one had assured me that it was a chronic weakness of all hospitals, and I must bear it. I did, armed with lavender water, with which I so besprinkled myself and premises, that I was soon known among my patients as "the nurse with the bottle." Having been run over by three excited surgeons, bumped against by migratory coal-hods, water-pails, and small boys, nearly scalded by an avalanche of newly-filled tea-pots, and hopelessly entangled in a knot of colored sisters coming to wash, I progressed by slow stages up stairs and down, till the main hall was reached, and I paused to take breath and a survey. There they were! "our brave boys," as the papers justly call them, for cowards could hardly have been so riddled with shot and shell, so torn and shattered, nor have borne suffering for which we have no name, with an uncomplaining fortitude, which made one glad to cherish each like a brother. In they came, some on stretchers, some in men's arms, some feebly staggering along propped on rude crutches, and one lay stark and still with covered face, as a comrade gave his name to be recorded before they carried him away to the dead house. All was hurry and confusion; the hall was full of these wrecks of humanity, for the most exhausted could not reach a bed till duly ticketed and registered; the walls were lined with rows of such as could sit, the floor covered with the more disabled, the steps and doorways filled with helpers and lookers on; the sound of many feet and voices made that usually quiet hour as noisy as noon; and, in the midst of it all, the matron's motherly face brought more comfort to many a poor soul, than the cordial draughts she administered, or the cheery words that welcomed all, making of the hospital a home.

The sight of several stretchers, each with its legless, armless, or desperately wounded occupant, entering my ward, admonished me that I was there to work, not to wonder or weep; so I corked up my feelings, and returned to the path of duty, which was rather "a hard road to travel" just then. The house had been a hotel before hospitals were needed, and many of the doors still bore their old names; some not so inappropriate as might be imagined, for that ward was in truth a *ball-room,* if gun-shot wounds could christen it. Forty beds were prepared, many already tenanted by tired men who fell down anywhere, and drowsed till the smell of food roused them. Round the great stove was gathered the dreariest group I ever saw— ragged, gaunt and pale, mud to the knees, with bloody bandages untouched since put on days before; many bundled up in blankets, coats being lost or useless; and all wearing that disheartened look which proclaimed defeat, more plainly than any telegram of the Burnside blunder. I pitied them so much, I dared not speak to them, though, remembering all they had been through since the fight at Fredericksburg, I yearned to serve the dreariest of them all. Presently, Miss Blank tore me from my refuge behind piles of one-sleeved shirts, odd socks, bandages and lint; put basin, sponge, towels, and a block of brown soap into my hands, with these appalling directions:

"Come, my dear, begin to wash as fast as you can. Tell them to take off socks, coats and shirts, scrub them well, put on clean shirts, and the attendants will finish them off, and lay them in bed."

If she had requested me to shave them all, or dance a hornpipe on the stove funnel, I should have been less staggered; but to scrub some dozen lords of creation at a moment's notice, was really— really——. However, there was no time for nonsense, and, having resolved when I came to do everything I was bid, I drowned my scruples in my washbowl, clutched my soap manfully, and, assuming a businesslike air, made a dab at the first dirty specimen I saw, bent on performing my task *vi et armis* if necessary. I chanced to light on a withered old Irishman, wounded in the head, which caused that portion of his frame to be tastefully laid out like a garden, the bandages being the walks, his hair the shrubbery. He was so overpowered by the honor of having a lady wash him, as he expressed it, that he did nothing but roll up his eyes, and bless me, in an irresistible style which was too much for my sense of the ludicrous; so we laughed together, and when I knelt down to take off his shoes, he "flopped" also, and wouldn't hear of my touching "them dirty craters. May your bed above be aisy darlin', for the day's work ye are doon!—Whoosh! there ye are, and bedad, it's hard tellin' which is the dirtiest, the fut or the shoe." It was; and if he hadn't been to the fore, I should have gone on pulling, under the impression that the "fut" was a boot, for trousers, socks, shoes and legs were a mass of mud. This comical tableau produced a general grin, at which propitious beginning I took heart and scrubbed away like any tidy parent on a Saturday night. Some of them took the performance like sleepy children, leaning their tired heads against me as I worked, others looked grimly scandalized, and several of the roughest colored like bashful girls. One wore a soiled little bag about his neck, and, as I moved it, to bathe his wounded breast, I said,

"Your talisman didn't save you, did it?"

"Well, I reckon it did, marm, for that shot would a gone a couple a inches deeper but for my old mammy's camphor bag," answered the cheerful philosopher.

Another, with a gun-shot wound through the cheek, asked for a looking-glass, and when I brought one, regarded his swollen face with a dolorous expression, as he muttered—

"I vow to gosh, that's too bad! I warn't a bad looking chap before, and now I'm done for; won't there be a thunderin' scar? and what on earth will Josephine Skinner say?"

He looked up at me with his one eye so appealingly, that I controlled my risibles, and assured him that if Josephine was a girl of sense, she would admire the honorable scar, as a lasting proof that he had faced the enemy, for all women thought a wound the best decoration a brave soldier could wear. I hope Miss Skinner verified the good opinion I so rashly expressed of her, but I shall never know.

The next scrubbee was a nice-looking lad, with a curly brown mane, honest blue eyes, and a merry mouth. He lay on a bed, with one leg gone, and the right arm so shattered that it must evidently follow: yet the little sergeant was as merry as if his afflictions were not worth lamenting over; and when a drop or two of salt water mingled with my suds at the sight of this strong young body, so marred and maimed, the boy looked up, with a brave smile, though there was a little quiver of the lips, as he said,

"Now don't you fret yourself about me, miss; I'm first rate here, for it's nuts to lie still on this bed, after knocking about in those confounded ambulances, that shake what there is left of a fellow to

jelly. I never was in one of these places before, and think this clean-
ing up a jolly thing for us, though I'm afraid it isn't for you ladies."

"Is this your first battle, Sergeant?"

"No, miss; I've been in six scrimmages, and never got a scratch
till this last one; but it's done the business pretty thoroughly for me,
I should say. Lord! what a scramble there'll be for arms and legs,
when we old boys come out of our graves, on the Judgment Day:
wonder if we shall get our own again? If we do, my leg will have to
tramp from Fredericksburg, my arm from here, I suppose, and meet
my body, wherever it may be."

The fancy seemed to tickle him mightily, for he laughed blithely,
and so did I; which, no doubt, caused the new nurse to be regarded
as a light-minded sinner by the Chaplain, who roamed vaguely
about, with his hands in his pockets, preaching resignation to cold,
hungry, wounded men, and evidently feeling himself, what he certainly was, the wrong man in the wrong place.

"I say, Mrs.!" called a voice behind me; and, turning, I saw a
rough Michigander, with an arm blown off at the shoulder, and two
or three bullets still in him—as he afterwards mentioned, as care-
lessly as if gentlemen were in the habit of carrying such trifles about
with them. I went to him, and, while administering a dose of soap
and water, he whispered, irefully:

"That red-headed devil, over yonder, is a reb, hang him! He's got
shet of a foot, or he'd a cut like the rest of the lot. Don't you wash
him, nor feed him, but jest let him holler till he's tired. It's a blasted
shame to fetch them fellers in here, along side of us; and so I'll tell
the chap that bosses this concern; cuss me if I don't."

I regret to say that I did not deliver a moral sermon upon the
duty of forgiving our enemies, and the sin of profanity, then and
there; but, being a red-hot Abolitionist, stared fixedly at the tall
rebel, who was a copperhead, in every sense of the word, and privately resolved to put soap in his eyes, rub his nose the wrong way,
and excoriate his cuticle generally, if I had the washing of him.

My amiable intentions, however, were frustrated; for, when I ap-
proached, with as Christian an expression as my principles would
allow, and asked the question—"Shall I try to make you more comfortable, sir?" all I got for my pains was a gruff—

"No; I'll do it myself."

"Here's your Southern chivalry, with a witness," thought I, dumping the basin down before him, thereby quenching a strong desire to give him a summary baptism, in return for his ungraciousness; for my angry passions rose, at this rebuff, in a way that would have scandalized good Dr. Watts. He was a disappointment in all respects, (the rebel, not the blessed Doctor,) for he was neither fiendish, romantic, pathetic, or anything interesting; but a long, fat man, with a head like a burning bush, and a perfectly expressionless face: so I could dislike him without the slightest drawback, and ignored his existence from that day forth. One redeeming trait he certainly did possess, as the floor speedily testified; for his ablutions were so vigorously performed, that his bed soon stood like an isolated island, in a sea of soap-suds, and he resembled a dripping merman, suffering from the loss of a fin. If cleanliness is a near neighbor to godliness, then was the big rebel the godliest man in my ward that day.

Having done up our human wash, and laid it out to dry, the second syllable of our version of the word War-fare was enacted with much success. Great trays of bread, meat, soup and coffee appeared; and both nurses and attendants turned waiters, serving bountiful rations to all who could eat. I can call my pinafore to testify to my good will in the work, for in ten minutes it was reduced to a perambulating bill of fare, presenting samples of all the refreshments going or gone. It was a lively scene; the long room lined with rows of beds, each filled by an occupant, whom water, shears, and clean raiment, had transformed from a dismal ragamuffin into a recumbent hero, with a cropped head. To and fro rushed matrons, maids, and convalescent "boys," skirmishing with knives and forks; retreating with empty plates; marching and counter-marching, with unvaried success, while the clash of busy spoons made most inspiring music for the charge of our Light Brigade:

> "Beds to the front of them,
> Beds to the right of them,
> Beds to the left of them,
> Nobody blundered.

> Beamed at by hungry souls,
> Screamed at with brimming bowls,
> Steamed at by army rolls,
>   Buttered and sundered.
> With coffee not cannon plied,
> Each must be satisfied,
> Whether they lived or died;
>   All the men wondered."

Very welcome seemed the generous meal, after a week of suffering, exposure, and short commons; soon the brown faces began to smile, as food, warmth, and rest, did their pleasant work; and the grateful "Thankee's" were followed by more graphic accounts of the battle and retreat, than any paid reporter could have given us. Curious contrasts of the tragic and comic met one everywhere; and some touching as well as ludicrous episodes, might have been recorded that day. A six foot New Hampshire man, with a leg broken and perforated by a piece of shell, so large that, had I not seen the wound, I should have regarded the story as a Munchausenism, beckoned me to come and help him, as he could not sit up, and both his bed and beard were getting plentifully anointed with soup. As I fed my big nestling with corresponding mouthfuls, I asked him how he felt during the battle.

"Well, 'twas my fust, you see, so I aint ashamed to say I was a trifle flustered in the beginnin', there was such an allfired racket; for ef there's anything I do spleen agin, it's noise. But when my mate, Eph Sylvester, fell, with a bullet through his head, I got mad, and pitched in, licketty cut. Our part of the fight didn't last long; so a lot of us larked round Fredericksburg, and give some of them houses a pretty consid'able of a rummage, till we was ordered out of the mess. Some of our fellows cut like time; but I warn't a-goin to run for nobody; and, fust thing I knew, a shell bust, right in front of us, and I keeled over, feelin' as if I was blowed higher'n a kite. I sung out, and the boys come back for me, double quick; but the way they chucked me over them fences was a caution, I tell you. Next day I was most as black as that darkey yonder, lickin' plates on the sly. This is bully coffee, ain't it? Give us another pull at it, and I'll be obleeged to you."

I did; and, as the last gulp subsided, he said, with a rub of his old handkerchief over eyes as well as mouth:

"Look a here; I've got a pair a earbobs and a handkercher pin I'm a goin' to give you, if you'll have them; for you're the very moral o' Lizy Sylvester, poor Eph's wife: that's why I signalled you to come over here. They aint much, I guess, but they'll do to memorize the rebs by."

Burrowing under his pillow, he produced a little bundle of what he called "truck," and gallantly presented me with a pair of earrings, each representing a cluster of corpulent grapes, and the pin a basket of astonishing fruit, the whole large and coppery enough for a small warming-pan. Feeling delicate about depriving him of such valuable relics, I accepted the earrings alone, and was obliged to depart, somewhat abruptly, when my friend stuck the warming-pan in the bosom of his night-gown, viewing it with much complacency, and, perhaps, some tender memory, in that rough heart of his, for the comrade he had lost.

Observing that the man next him had left his meal untouched, I offered the same service I had performed for his neighbor, but he shook his head.

"Thank you, ma'am; I don't think I'll ever eat again, for I'm shot in the stomach. But I'd like a drink of water, if you aint too busy."

I rushed away, but the water-pails were gone to be refilled, and it was some time before they reappeared. I did not forget my patient patient, meanwhile, and, with the first mugful, hurried back to him. He seemed asleep; but something in the tired white face caused me to listen at his lips for a breath. None came. I touched his forehead; it was cold: and then I knew that, while he waited, a better nurse than I had given him a cooler draught, and healed him with a touch. I laid the sheet over the quiet sleeper, whom no noise could now disturb; and, half an hour later, the bed was empty. It seemed a poor requital for all he had sacrificed and suffered,—that hospital bed, lonely even in a crowd; for there was no familiar face for him to look his last upon; no friendly voice to say, Good bye; no hand to lead him gently down into the Valley of the Shadow; and he vanished, like a drop in that red sea upon whose shores so many women stand lamenting. For a moment I felt bitterly indignant at this seeming carelessness of the value of life, the sanctity of death; then consoled myself with the thought that, when the great muster roll was called, these nameless men might be promoted above many whose tall monuments record the barren honors they have won.

All having eaten, drank, and rested, the surgeons began their rounds; and I took my first lesson in the art of dressing wounds. It wasn't a festive scene, by any means; for Dr P., whose Aid I constituted myself, fell to work with a vigor which soon convinced me that I was a weaker vessel, though nothing would have induced me to confess it then. He had served in the Crimea, and seemed to regard a dilapidated body very much as I should have regarded a damaged garment; and, turning up his cuffs, whipped out a very unpleasant looking housewife, cutting, sawing, patching and piecing, with the enthusiasm of an accomplished surgical seamstress; explaining the process, in scientific terms, to the patient, meantime; which, of course, was immensely cheering and comfortable. There was an uncanny sort of fascination in watching him, as he peered and probed into the mechanism of those wonderful bodies, whose mysteries he understood so well. The more intricate the wound, the better he liked it. A poor private, with both legs off, and shot through the lungs, possessed more attractions for him than a dozen generals, slightly scratched in some "masterly retreat;" and had any one appeared in small pieces, requesting to be put together again, he would have considered it a special dispensation.

The amputations were reserved till the morrow, and the merciful magic of ether was not thought necessary that day, so the poor souls had to bear their pains as best they might. It is all very well to talk of the patience of woman; and far be it from me to pluck that feather from her cap, for, heaven knows, she isn't allowed to wear many; but the patient endurance of these men, under trials of the flesh, was truly wonderful. Their fortitude seemed contagious, and scarcely a cry escaped them, though I often longed to groan for them, when pride kept their white lips shut, while great drops stood upon their foreheads, and the bed shook with the irrepressible tremor of their tortured bodies. One or two Irishmen anathematized the doctors with the frankness of their nation, and ordered the Virgin to stand by them, as if she had been the wedded Biddy to whom they could administer the poker, if she didn't; but, as a general thing, the work went on in silence, broken only by some quiet request for roller, instruments, or plaster, a sigh from the patient, or a sympathizing murmur from the nurse.

It was long past noon before these repairs were even partially made; and, having got the bodies of my boys into something like order, the next task was to minister to their minds, by writing letters to the anxious souls at home; answering questions, reading papers, taking possession of money and valuables; for the eighth commandment was reduced to a very fragmentary condition, both by the blacks and whites, who ornamented our hospital with their presence. Pocket books, purses, miniatures, and watches, were sealed up, labelled, and handed over to the matron, till such times as the owners thereof were ready to depart homeward or campward again. The letters dictated to me, and revised by me, that afternoon, would have made an excellent chapter for some future history of the war; for, like that which Thackeray's "Ensign Spooney" wrote his mother just before Waterloo, they were "full of affection, pluck, and bad spelling;" nearly all giving lively accounts of the battle, and ending with a somewhat sudden plunge from patriotism to provender, desiring "Marm," "Mary Ann," or "Aunt Peters," to send along some pies, pickles, sweet stuff, and apples, "to yourn in haste," Joe, Sam, or Ned, as the case might be.

My little Sergeant insisted on trying to scribble something with his left hand, and patiently accomplished some half dozen lines of hieroglyphics, which he gave me to fold and direct, with a boyish blush, that rendered a glimpse of "My Dearest Jane," unnecessary, to assure me that the heroic lad had been more successful in the service of Commander-in-Chief Cupid than that of Gen. Mars; and a charming little romance blossomed instanter in Nurse Periwinkle's romantic fancy, though no further confidences were made that day, for Sergeant fell asleep, and, judging from his tranquil face, visited his absent sweetheart in the pleasant land of dreams.

At five o'clock a great bell rang, and the attendants flew, not to arms, but to their trays, to bring up supper, when a second uproar announced that it was ready. The new comers woke at the sound; and I presently discovered that it took a very bad wound to incapacitate the defenders of the faith for the consumption of their rations; the amount that some of them sequestered was amazing; but when I suggested the probability of a famine hereafter, to the matron, that motherly lady cried out: "Bless their hearts, why shouldn't they eat? It's their only amusement; so fill every one, and, if there's not enough ready to-night, I'll lend my share to the Lord by giving it to the boys." And, whipping up her coffee-pot and plate of toast, she gladdened the eyes and stomachs of two or three dissatisfied heroes, by serving them with a liberal hand; and I haven't the slightest doubt that, having cast her bread upon the waters, it came back buttered, as another large-hearted old lady was wont to say.

Then came the doctor's evening visit; the administration of medicines; washing feverish faces; smoothing tumbled beds; wetting wounds; singing lullabies; and preparations for the night. By twelve, the last labor of love was done; the last "good night" spoken; and, if any needed a reward for that day's work, they surely received it, in the silent eloquence of those long lines of faces, showing pale and peaceful in the shaded rooms, as we quitted them, followed by grateful glances that lighted us to bed, where rest, the sweetest, made our pillows soft, while Night and Nature took our places, filling that great house of pain with the healing miracles of Sleep, and his divine brother, Death.

6

Woman's Economic Role: Egalitarianism

Woman in the Nineteenth Century

(New York, 1845)

MARGARET FULLER

. . . By Man I mean both man and woman: these are the two halves of one thought. . . . I believe that the development of the one cannot be effected without that of the other. My highest wish is that this truth should be distinctly and rationally apprehended, and the conditions of life and freedom recognized as the same for the daughters and the sons of time; twin exponents of a divine thought.

. . . We would have every arbitrary barrier thrown down. We would have every path laid open to woman as freely as to man. Were this done and a slight temporary fermentation allowed to subside, we should see crystallizations more pure and of more various beauty. We believe the divine energy would pervade nature to a degree unknown in the history of former ages, and that no discordant collision, but a ravishing harmony of the spheres would ensue.

Yet, then and only then, will mankind be ripe for this, when inward and outward freedom for woman as much as for man shall be acknowledged as a right, not yielded as a concession. . . . man cannot, by right, lay even well-meant restrictions on woman. . . .

What woman needs is not as a woman to act or rule, but as a nature to grow, as an intellect to discern, as a soul to live freely and unimpeded, to unfold such powers as were given her when we left our common home. . . .

Where this thought of equality begins to diffuse itself, it is shown in four ways.

The household partnership. . . .

The man furnishes the house; the woman regulates it. Their relation is one of mutual esteem, mutual dependence. . . . This relation is good, as far as it goes.

. . . as the intellectual development of woman has spread wider and risen higher, they have, not unfrequently, shared the same employment. . . .

Women have taken possession of so many provinces for which men had pronounced them unfit, that though these still declare there are some inaccessible to them, it is difficult to say just *where* they must stop.

We must have units before we can have union. . . .

"The excellent woman is she, who, if the husband dies, can be a father to the children." And this, if read aright, tells a great deal.

. . . [Charles Fourier] places woman on an entire equality with man, and wishes to give to one as to the other that independence which must result from intellectual and practical development.

. . . I have aimed to show that no age was left entirely without a witness of the equality of the sexes in function, duty and hope. . . .

That now the time has come when a clearer vision and better action are possible. When man and woman may regard one another as brother and sister, the pillars of one porch, the priests of one worship.

I have believed and intimated that this hope would receive an ampler fruition, than ever before, in our own land.

And it will do so if this land carry out the principles from which sprang our national life.

. . . if you ask me what offices they may fill; I reply—any. I do not care what case you put; let them be sea-captains, if you will. I do not doubt there are women well fitted for such an office, and, if so, I should be glad to see them in it. . . .

I think women need, especially at this juncture, a much greater range of occupation than they have, to rouse their latent powers.

. . . [Fourier], in proposing a great variety of employments, in manufactures or the care of plants and animals, allows for one third of woman, as likely to have a taste for masculine pursuits, one third of men for feminine.

Petition of Abby May Alcott and Others to the Citizens of Massachusetts on Equal Political Rights of Woman

(*Una*, November 1853)

. . . Crowded now into few employments, women starve each other by close competition, and too often vice borrows overwhelming power of temptation from poverty. Open to women a great variety of employments, and her wages in each will rise; the energy and enterprise of the more highly endowed, will find full scope in honest effort, and the frightful vice of our cities will be stopped at the fountain-head. . . .

A Practical Illustration of "Woman's Right to Labor"

Or, A Letter from Marie E. Zakrzewska, M.D., . . . Edited
by Caroline H. Dall (Boston, 1860)

. . . Reflecting men are at this moment ready to help women to enter wider fields of labor, because, on the one side, the destitution and vice they have helped to create appalls their consciousness; and, on the other, a profane inanity stands a perpetual blasphemy in the face of the Most High.

One thing I felt profoundly: as men sow they must reap; and so must women. The practical misery of the world—its terrible impurity will never be abated till women prepare themselves from their earliest years to enter the arena of which they are ambitious, and stand there at last mature and calm, but, above all, *thoroughly trained;* trained also at *the side of the men,* with whom they must ultimately work; and not likely, therefore, to lose balance or fitness by being thrown, at the last moment, into unaccustomed relations. . . .

The object of my whole life has been to inspire in women a desire for *thorough training* to some special end, and a willingness to share the training of men both for specific and moral reasons. Only by sharing such training can women be sure that they will be well trained; only by God-ordained, natural communion of all men and women can the highest moral results be reached.

"Free labor and free society:" I have said often to myself, in these two phrases lies hidden the future purification of society. When men and women go everywhere together, the sights they dare not see together will no longer exist.

Fair and serene will rise before them all heights of possible attainment; and, looking off over the valleys of human endeavor together, they will clear the forest, drain the morass, and improve the interval, stirred by a common impulse. . . .

"How I Went Out to Service"

(*The Independent,* June 4, 1874)

L. M. ALCOTT

When I was eighteen I wanted something to do. I had tried teaching for two years, and hated it; I had tried sewing, and could not earn my bread in that way, at the cost of health; I tried story-writing and got five dollars for stories which now bring a hundred; I had thought seriously of going upon the stage, but certain highly respectable relatives were so shocked at the mere idea that I relinquished my dramatic aspirations.

"What *shall* I do?" was still the question that perplexed me. I was ready to work, eager to be independent, and too proud to endure patronage. But the right task seemed hard to find, and my bottled energies were fermenting in a way that threatened an explosion before long. . . .

NOTE: Alcott chose to go out to service, in this case a disastrous choice. After seven weeks of hard labor in the family of James Richardson of Dedham, Massachusetts, in 1851, she received four dollars in payment, which her family returned.

L. M. Alcott to James Redpath

(July? 1863)

. . . You ask about any other story I may have. . . . This one was begun with the design of putting some [of] my own experiences into a story illustrating the trials of young women who want employment & find it hard to get. From time to time I see articles on the same subject & various people have begged me to finish "Success" as I at first christened the book [which became *Work*].

The story is made up of various essays this girl makes, her failures & succes[s]es told in chapters merry or sad. . . .

"Happy Women"

(*New York Ledger*, April 11, 1868)

L. M. ALCOTT

One of the trials of woman-kind is the fear of being an old maid. To escape this dreadful doom, young girls rush into matrimony with a recklessness which astonishes the beholder; never pausing to remember that the loss of liberty, happiness, and self-respect is poorly repaid by the barren honor of being called "Mrs." instead of "Miss."

Fortunately, this foolish prejudice is fast disappearing, conquered by the success of a certain class belonging to the sisterhood. This class is composed of superior women who, from various causes, remain single, and devote themselves to some earnest work; espousing philanthropy, art, literature, music, medicine, or whatever task taste, necessity, or change suggests, and remaining as faithful to and as happy in their choice as married women with husbands and homes. It being my good fortune to know several such, I venture to offer a little sketch of them to those of my young countrywomen who, from choice or necessity, stand alone, seeking to find the happiness which is the right of all.

Here is L., a rich man's daughter; pretty, accomplished, sensible, and good. She tried fashionable life and found that it did not satisfy her. No lover was happy enough to make a response in her heart, and at twenty-three she looked about her for something to occupy and interest her. She was attracted towards the study of medicine; became absorbed in it; went alone to Paris and London; studied faithfully; received her diploma, and, having practised successfully for a time, was appointed the resident physician of a city hospital. Here, doing a truly womanly work, she finds no time for ennui, unhappiness, or the vague longing for something to fill heart and life, which leads so many women to take refuge in frivolous or dangerous amusements and pursuits. She never talks of her mission or her rights, but beautifully fulfils the one and quietly assumes the others. Few criticise or condemn her course, and none question her success. Respected and beloved by all who know her, she finds genuine satisfaction in her work, and is the busiest, happiest, most useful woman whom I know.

Next comes M., a brilliant, talented girl, full of energy, ambition, and noble aspirations. Poor, yet attractive, through natural gifts and graces, to her came the great temptation of such a girl's life—a rich lover; an excellent young man, but her inferior in all respects. She felt this, and so did he, but hoping that love would make them equals, he urged his suit.

"If I loved him," she said, "my way would be plain, and I should not hesitate a minute. But I do not; I've tried, and I am sure I *never* can feel toward him as I should. It is a great temptation, for I long to cultivate my talent to help my family, to see the world, and enjoy life, and all this may be done if I said 'Yes.' People tell me that I am foolish to reject this good fortune; that it is my duty to accept it; that I shall get on very well without love, and talk as if it were a business transaction. It is hard to say 'No'; but I *must,* for in marriage I want to look up, not down. I cannot make it seem right to take this offer, and I must let it go, for I dare not sell my liberty."

She made her choice, turned away from the pleasant future laid before her, and took up her load again. With her one talent in her hand she faced poverty, cheerfully teaching music, year after year; hoping always, complaining never, and finding herself a stronger, happier woman for that act: A richer woman also; for, though the husband was lost a true friend was gained—since the lover, with respect added to his love, said manfully, "She is right; God bless her!"

S. is poor, plain, ungifted, and ordinary in all things but one—a cheerful, helpful spirit, that loves its neighbor better than itself, and cannot rest till it has proved its sincerity. Few, so placed, would have lived forty hard, dull years without becoming either sharp and sour, or bitter and blue. But S. is as sweet and sunny as a child; and, to those who know her, the personification of content. The only talent she possesses is that of loving every helpless, suffering, forlorn and outcast creature whom she meets. Finding her round of home duties too small for her benevolence, she became one of the home missionaries, whose reports are never read, whose salaries are never paid of earth. Poverty-stricken homes, sick-beds, sinful souls, and sorrowing hearts attract her as irresistibly as pleasure attracts other women, and she faithfully ministers to such, unknown and unrewarded.

"I never had a lover, and I never can have you know. I'm *so* plain," she says, with a smile that is pathetic in its humility, its unconscious wistfulness.

She is mistaken here; for there are many to whom that plain face is beautiful, that helpful hand very dear. Her lovers are not of the romantic sort; but old women, little children, erring men, and forlorn girls give her an affection as endearing and sincere as any husband could have done. Few will know her worth here, but, in the long hereafter, I am sure S. will be blest with eternal beauty, happiness, and love.

A. is a woman of a strongly individual type, who in the course of an unusually varied experience has seen so much of what a wise man has called "the tragedy of modern married life," that she is afraid to try it. Knowing that for one of a peculiar nature like herself such an experiment would be doubly hazardous, she has obeyed instinct and become a chronic old maid. Filial and fraternal love must satisfy her, and grateful that such ties are possible, she lives for them and is content. Literature is a fond and faithful spouse, and the little family that has sprung up around her, though perhaps unlovely and uninteresting to others, is a profitable source of satisfaction to her maternal heart. After a somewhat tempestuous voyage, she is glad to find herself in a quiet haven whence she can look back upon her vanished youth and feel that though the blossom time of life is past, a little fruit remains to ripen in the early autumn coming on. Not lonely, for parents, brothers and sisters, friends and babies keep her heart full and warm; not idle, for necessity, stern, yet kindly teacher, has taught her the worth of work; not unhappy, for love and labor, like good angels, walk at either hand, and the divine Friend fills the world with strength and beauty for the soul and eyes that have learned to see it thankfully.

My sisters, don't be afraid of the words, "old maid," for it is in your power to make this a term of honor, not reproach. It is not necessary to be a sour, spiteful spinster, with nothing to do but brew tea, talk scandal and tend a pocket-handkerchief. No, the world is full of work, needing all the heads, hearts, and hands we can bring to do it. Never was there so splendid an opportunity for women to enjoy their liberty and prove that they deserve it by using it wisely. If love comes as it should come, accept it in God's name and be worthy of His best blessing. If it never comes, then in God's name reject the shadow of it, for that can never satisfy a hungry heart. Do not be ashamed to own the truth—do not be daunted by the fear of ridicule and loneliness, nor saddened by the loss of a woman's tenderest ties. Be true to yourselves; cherish whatever talent you possess, and in using it faithfully for the good of others you will most assuredly find happiness for yourself, and make of life no failure, but a beautiful success.

Work: A Story of Experience

(Boston, 1873)

L. M. ALCOTT

". . . I'm not going to sit and wait for any man to give me independence, if I can earn it for myself."

Christie was one of that large class of women who, moderately endowed with talents, earnest and true-hearted, are driven by necessity, temperament, or principle out into the world to find support, happiness, and homes for themselves. Many turn back discouraged; more accept shadow for substance, and discover their mistake too late; the weakest lose their purpose and themselves; but the strongest struggle on, and, after danger and defeat, earn at last the best success this world can give us, the possession of a brave and cheerful spirit, rich in self-knowledge, self-control, self-help. This was the real desire of Christie's heart; . . . and to this happy end she was slowly yet surely brought by the long discipline of life and labor.

. . . Such women were much needed and are not always easy to find; for even in democratic America the hand that earns its daily bread must wear some talent, name, or honor as an ornament, before it is very cordially shaken by those that wear white gloves.

"Perhaps this is the task my life has been fitting me for," she said. ". . . This new task seems to offer me the chance of being among the pioneers, to do the hard work, share the persecution, and help lay the foundation of a new emancipation whose happy success I may never see."

. . . "I am not tired yet: I hope I never shall be, for without my work I should fall into despair or *ennui*. There is so much to be done, and it is so delightful to help do it, that I never mean to fold my hands till they are useless. I owe all I can do, for in labor, and the efforts and experiences that grew out of it, I have found independence, education, happiness, and religion."

ℒ. ℳ. Alcott to Maria S. Porter

(1874)

I rejoice greatly therat, and hope that the first thing that you and Mrs. Sewall propose in your first meeting will be to reduce the salary of the head master of the High School, and increase the salary of the first woman assistant, whose work is quite as good as his, and even harder, to make the pay equal. I believe in the same pay for the same good work. Don't you? In future let woman do whatever she can do; let men place no more impediments in the way; above all things let's have fair play,—let *simple justice* be done, say I. Let us hear no more of "woman's sphere" either from our wise (?) legislators beneath the State House dome, or from our clergymen in their pulpits. I am tired, year after year, of hearing such twaddle about sturdy oaks and clinging vines and man's chivalric protection of woman. Let woman find her own limitations, and if, as is so confidently asserted, nature has defined her sphere, she will be guided accordingly, but in heaven's name give her a chance! Let the professions be open to her; let fifty years of college education be hers, and then we shall see what we shall see. Then, and not until then, shall we be able to say what woman can and what she cannot do, and coming generations will know and be able to define more clearly what is a "woman's sphere" than these benighted men who now try to do it.

Rose in Bloom. A Sequel to "Eight Cousins"

(Boston, 1876)

L. M. ALCOTT

. . . Rose's voice was heard saying very earnestly,—

"Now you have all told your plans for the future, why don't you ask us ours?"

"Because we know that there is only one thing for a pretty girl to do,—break a dozen or so of hearts before she finds one to suit, then marry and settle," answered Charlie, as if no other reply was possible.

"That may be the case with many, but not with us, for Phebe and I believe that it is as much a right and a duty for women to do something with their lives as for men; and we are not going to be satisfied with such frivolous parts as you give us," cried Rose, with kindling eyes. "I mean what I say, and you cannot laugh me down. Would *you* be contented to be told to enjoy yourself for a little while, then marry and do nothing more till you die?" she added, turning to Archie.

"Of course not: that is only a part of a man's life," he answered decidedly.

"A very precious and lovely part, but not *all*," continued Rose; "neither should it be for a woman: for we've got minds and souls as well as hearts; ambition and talents, as well as beauty and accomplishments; and we want to live and learn as well as love and be loved. I'm sick of being told that is all a woman is fit for! I won't have any thing to do with love till I prove that I am something beside a housekeeper and baby-tender!"

"Heaven preserve us! here's woman's rights with a vengeance!"

cried Charlie, starting up with mock horror, while the others regarded Rose with mingled surprise and amusement, evidently fancying it all a girlish outbreak.

"Ah, you needn't pretend to be shocked: you will be in earnest presently; for this is only the beginning of my strong-mindedness," continued Rose. . . .

7

Sex and Feminism

The Young Wife

(Boston, 1838)

WILLIAM ANDRUS ALCOTT

LOVE.

Is it necessary for love to decline after marriage? Internal love increases. Means of increasing it. Doing good to others makes us love them. Anecdotes; the little girl—the deist. Love, a matter within our own control. General rule. Cautions.

It would excite a smile were I to exhort you, in so many words, to love your husbands. And yet I fear that, in too many instances, no exhortation is more needed. I fear that as society is now constituted, the love of many a young wife is very far from being what it ought to be.

There is a very general opinion abroad, that the love of husband and wife must, after marriage, necessarily begin to decline. Or if it can be kept up at all, that it can only be done by special or extraordinary exertion. This, in my view, is a great mistake.

I know there is a species of love, if it deserves the name, which declines soon after marriage; and it is no matter if it does. If there is nothing but this which attracts a young couple—if the love which has drawn them into matrimony is merely a personal, or I would rather say an external love—if the parties are neither of them bound by any mental or moral attraction, the sooner we are undeceived in a matter of such unspeakable moment, the better.

There can be no objection to external love, where it is a mere accompaniment of that which is internal. What I object to, is the making too much of it; or giving it a place in our heart which is disproportioned to its real value. Our affections should rather be based chiefly on sweetness of temper, intelligence and moral excellency. It is the internal which we should chiefly regard, and not the external, except in so far as the latter is an appropriate index of the former.

This internal love it is which will form the subject of the present chapter. It is this which I wish to have kept up and increased in the matrimonial relation. It is this to which I refer when I say, love your husbands. It is this which, instead of declining, may be made, to use language which has been appropriated to another and still more important subject, to burn brighter and brighter "unto the perfect day."

A capital mistake has been often made in regard to the means of inducing or increasing love. "It is more blessed to give than to receive," is the scripture rule; but this has been too generally inverted, and mankind have seemed to act on the principle that it is more blessed to receive than to give.

Let me be fully understood. My paraphrase of the scripture doctrine above quoted would be the following—"We love those to whom we do good, more than we love those who do good to us;" and mankind, by their practice, seem to have inverted it. They seem to take it for granted, that we love those who do good to us more than we love those to whom we do good.

Nowhere, in practical life, is this mistake more common than in the matrimonial relation, especially in its early stages. The husband, in order to secure the affection of his companion, bestows on her a thousand little attentions and favors. He supposes that if it gratifies her to receive them, her affection will increase in proportion to their frequency, and the pleasure they seem to afford her. And the wife sometimes bestows her little attentions upon him on the same principle.

Now I do not undertake to say or intimate that such is not, in any degree, the result—for I believe quite otherwise. Indeed, we are not told that we do not love at all those who do good to us, but only that the love of the receiver is not increased by the gift in as great a degree, or rather as rapidly, as that of the giver.

If, therefore, you find there is any danger that the external attachment you have formed for your husband is beginning to decline, do not hastily conclude that there is anything wrong—anything which has been misapprehended—in forming the relation. It may be a favorable omen. It certainly will be, if its place is fully supplied by that internal attachment of which I have just now been speaking, and which is the result of doing good.

In this view, as I have already said, you have it in your power to increase the flame of internal love towards him to whom you have consented to stand as an "help-meet," and to an extent to which it is impossible to assign any limits. Wherever you are, and how great soever the attachment between you, and whether, for aught I know, in this state of existence or any other, you may calculate on an ability to increase his happiness and your own love. The secret consists in doing him good.

As to the appropriate means and methods of doing him good, it seems at first view almost unnecessary for me to say one word. And yet I am willing to do so; for there may be those who will not regard me as tedious. I shall not indeed presume to point out the particular ways and means in which a young wife can do good to her husband, but only to give a few hints. Some of these means have been set forth at full length, in preceding chapters; and others will be involved in the treatment of other topics, in chapters to follow.

One general rule may here be laid down, which is—"Do everything for your husband which your strength and a due regard to your health will admit." I will not say that it were not wise, sometimes, to go even beyond your strength—to deny yourself—and even to make a self-sacrifice. But I do insist on your going to the borders, at least, of self-denial and self-sacrifice.

Such advice, at first view, may seem to be unreasonable. It may be said that I would make woman a slave. No such thing: I would make her a christian—and a happy one. I would give her that freedom to which christianity, with its high hopes and promises, bids her to aspire.

She will not long be compelled to be a menial to her husband. He must be a brute, and worse than a brute, whom such a course of active devoted service will not arouse to corresponding action. I am not ignorant of the fact that, in some instances, the more we do for others, the more they will allow us to do for them; and that what is at first considered on all hands as gratuitous on our part, they will ere long, if continued, claim as their due.

But it is seldom thus in the matrimonial relation. Few who bear the shape, and none who have the souls of men, will permit a wife to continue long to do everything in the way I have mentioned. They will yield, and be led gradually to imbibe the same spirit. When this is done—when the husband and wife both strive to do everything in their power for each other—then will they have attained a high degree of felicity. Then, too, will they have secured, most effectually, the power to rise still higher, and to love each other more and more ardently.

It is an almost universal custom to act on the other principle—to do nothing for each other, as we pass along the road of matrimonial life, which we can help—that, like a canker, slowly eats out the life-blood of domestic happiness. Oh that husbands—but I write not now for them—oh that wives were universally wise on this subject; and that they would consider well the tendencies of these things. If I am right, there is much error abroad on this subject, and in few things is a reform more necessary.

But, it is said, we must be content to wait, with patience, for results; that we must not expect too much of the world immediately; and that woman will be elevated slowly, in the progress of things, without extra effort. It may be so. We hope it will be so. But I do not expect it, nor are expectations of this kind founded in a knowledge of human nature as it is, or as it ever has been.

Woman in the Nineteenth Century

(New York, 1845)

MARGARET FULLER

Male and female represent the two sides of the great radical dualism. But, in fact, they are perpetually passing into one another. Fluid hardens to solid, solid rushes to fluid. There is no wholly masculine man, no purely feminine woman. . . .

Man partakes of the feminine in the Apollo, woman of the masculine as Minerva. . . .

Do not rejoice in conquests, either that your power to allure may be seen by other women, or for the pleasure of rousing passionate feelings that gratify your love of excitement.

It must happen, no doubt, that frank and generous women will excite love they do not reciprocate, but, in nine cases out of ten, the woman has, half consciously, done much to excite. In this case she shall not be held guiltless, either as to the unhappiness or injury to the lover. Pure love, inspired by a worthy object, must ennoble and bless, whether mutual or not. . . .

That her hand may be given with dignity, she must be able to stand alone. . . .

A profound thinker has said, "no married woman can represent the female world, for she belongs to her husband. The idea of woman must be represented by a virgin."

But that is the very fault of marriage, and of the present relation between the sexes, that the woman does belong to the man, instead of forming a whole with him. Were it otherwise, there would be no such limitation to the thought. . . .

"Taming a Tartar"

(*Frank Leslie's Illustrated Newspaper,*
November 30–December 21, 1867)

L. M. ALCOTT

CHAPTER I

"Dear Mademoiselle, I assure you it is an arrangement both profitable and agreeable to one, who, like you, desires change of occupation and scene, as well as support. Madame la Princesse is most
affable, generous, and to those who please her, quite child-like in
her affection."

"But, madame, am I fit for the place? Does it not need accomplishments and graces which I do not possess? There is a wide difference between being a teacher in a *Pensionnat pour Demoiselles* like
this and the companion of a princess."

"Ah, hah, my dear, it is nothing. Let not the fear of rank disturb
you; these Russians are but savages, and all their money, splendor,
and the polish Paris gives them, do not suffice to change the barbar-
ians. You are the superior in breeding as in intelligence, as you will
soon discover; and for accomplishments, yours will bear the test
anywhere. I grant you Russians have much talent for them, and ac-
quire with marvelous ease, but taste they have not, nor the skill to
use these weapons as we use them."

"The princess is an invalid, you say?"

"Yes; but she suffers little, is delicate and needs care, amusement,
yet not excitement. You are to chat with her, to read, sing, strive to
fill the place of confidante. She sees little society, and her wing of
the hotel is quite removed from that of the prince, who is one of the
lions just now."

"Is it of him they tell the strange tales of his princely generosity, his fearful temper, childish caprices, and splendid establishment?"

"In truth, yes; Paris is wild for him, as for some magnificent savage beast. Madame la Comtesse Millefleur declared that she never knew whether he would fall at her feet, or annihilate her, so impetuous were his moods. At one moment showing all the complaisance and elegance of a born Parisian, the next terrifying the beholders by some outburst of savage wrath, some betrayal of the Tartar blood that is in him. Ah! it is incredible how such things amaze one."

"Has the princess the same traits? If so, I fancy the situation of companion is not easy to fill."

"No, no, she is not of the same blood. She is a half-sister; her mother was a Frenchwoman; she was educated in France, and lived here till her marriage with Prince Tcherinski. She detests St. Petersburg, adores Paris, and hopes to keep her brother here till the spring, for the fearful climate of the north is death to her delicate lungs. She is a gay, simple, confiding person; a child still in many things, and since her widowhood entirely under the control of this brother, who loves her tenderly, yet is a tyrant to her as to all who approach him."

I smiled as my loquacious friend gave me these hints of my future master and mistress, but in spite of all drawbacks, I liked the prospect, and what would have deterred another, attracted me. I was alone in the world, fond of experiences and adventures, self-reliant and self-possessed; eager for change, and anxious to rub off the rust of five years' servitude in Madame Bayard's Pensionnat. This new occupation pleased me, and but for a slight fear of proving unequal to it, I should have at once accepted madame's proposition. She knew everyone, and through some friend had heard of the princess's wish to find an English lady as companion and teacher, for a whim had seized her to learn English. Madame knew I intended to leave her, my health and spirits being worn by long and arduous duties, and she kindly interested herself to secure the place for me.

"Go then, dear mademoiselle, make a charming toilet and present yourself to the princess without delay, or you lose your opportunity. I have smoothed the way for you; your own address will do the rest, and in one sense, your fortune is made, if all goes well."

I obeyed madame, and when I was ready, took a critical survey of myself, trying to judge of the effect upon others. The long mirror showed me a slender, well-molded figure, and a pale face—not beautiful, but expressive, for the sharply cut, somewhat haughty features betrayed good blood, spirit and strength. Gray eyes, large and lustrous, under straight, dark brows; a firm mouth and chin, proud nose, wide brow, with waves of chestnut hair parted plainly back into heavy coils behind. Five years in Paris had taught me the art of dress, and a good salary permitted me to indulge my taste. Although simply made, I flattered myself that my promenade costume of silk and sable was *en règle,* as well as becoming, and with a smile at myself in the mirror I went my way, wondering if this new plan was to prove the welcome change so long desired.

As the carriage drove into the court-yard of the prince's hotel in the Champs Élysées, and a gorgeous *laquais* carried up my card, my heart beat a little faster than usual, and when I followed the servant in, I felt as if my old life ended suddenly, and one of strange interest had already begun.

The princess was not ready to receive me yet, and I was shown into a splendid *salon* to wait. My entrance was noiseless, and as I took a seat, my eyes fell on the half-drawn curtains which divided the room from another. Two persons were visible, but as neither saw me in the soft gloom of the apartment, I had an opportunity to look as long and curiously as I pleased. The whole scene was as unlike those usually found in a Parisian *salon* as can well be imagined.

Though three o'clock in the afternoon, it was evidently early morning with the gentleman stretched on the ottoman, reading a novel and smoking a Turkish chibouk—for his costume was that of a Russian seigneur in *déshabillé.* A long Caucasian caftan of the finest white sheepskin, a pair of loose black velvet trowsers, bound round the waist by a rich shawl, and Kasan boots of crimson leather, ornamented with golden embroidery on the instep, covered a pair of feet which seemed disproportionately small compared to the unusually tall, athletic figure of the man; so also did the head with a red silk handkerchief bound over the thick black hair. The costume suited the face; swarthy, black-eyed, scarlet-lipped, heavybrowed and beardless, except a thick mustache; serfs wear beards, but Russian nobles never. A strange face, for even in repose the indescribable difference of race was visible; the contour of the head, molding of the features, hue of hair and skin, even the attitude, all betrayed a trace of the savage strength and spirit of one in whose veins flowed the blood of men reared in tents, and born to lead wild lives in a wild land.

This unexpected glance behind the scenes interested me much, and I took note of everything within my ken. The book which the slender brown hand held was evidently a French novel, but when a lap-dog disturbed the reader, it was ordered off in Russian with a sonorous oath, I suspect, and an impatient gesture. On a guéridon, or side-table, stood a velvet *porte-cigare,* a box of sweetmeats, a bottle of Bordeaux, and a tall glass of cold tea, with a slice of lemon floating in it. A musical instrument, something like a mandolin, lay near the ottoman, a piano stood open, with a sword and helmet on it, and sitting in a corner, noiselessly making cigarettes, was a half-grown boy, a serf I fancied, from his dress and the silent, slavish way in which he watched his master.

The princess kept me waiting long, but I was not impatient, and when I was summoned at last I could not resist a backward glance at the brilliant figure I left behind me. The servant's voice had roused him, and, rising to his elbow, he leaned forward to look, with an expression of mingled curiosity and displeasure in the largest, blackest eyes I ever met.

I found the princess, a pale, pretty little woman of not more than twenty, buried in costly furs, though the temperature of her boudoir seemed tropical to me. Most gracious was my reception, and at once all fear vanished, for she was as simple and wanting in dignity as any of my young pupils.

"Ah, Mademoiselle Varna, you come in good time to spare me from the necessity of accepting a lady whom I like not. She is excellent, but too grave; while you reassure me at once by that smile. Sit near me, and let us arrange the affair before my brother comes. You incline to give me your society, I infer from the good Bayard?"

"If Madame la Princesse accepts my services on trial for a time, I much desire to make the attempt, as my former duties have become irksome, and I have a great curiosity to see St. Petersburg."

"*Mon Dieu!* I trust it will be long before we return to that detestable climate. *Chère* mademoiselle, I entreat you to say nothing of this desire to my brother. He is mad to go back to his wolves, his ice and his barbarous delights; but I cling to Paris, for it is my life. In the spring it is inevitable, and I submit—but not now. If you come to me, I conjure you to aid me in delaying the return, and shall be forever grateful if you help to secure this reprieve for me."

So earnest and beseeching were her looks, her words, and so entirely did she seem to throw herself upon my sympathy and goodwill, that I could not but be touched and won, in spite of my surprise. I assured her that I would do my best, but could not flatter myself that any advice of mine would influence the prince.

"You do not know him; but from what Bayard tells me of your skill in controlling wayward wills and hot tempers, I feel sure that you can influence Alexis. In confidence, I tell you what you will soon learn, if you remain: that though the best and tenderest of brothers, the prince is hard to manage, and one must tread cautiously in approaching him. His will is iron; and a decree once uttered is as irrevocable as the laws of the Medes and Persians. He has always claimed entire liberty for himself, entire obedience from every one about him; and my father's early death leaving him the head of our house, confirmed these tyrannical tendencies. To keep him in Paris is my earnest desire, and in order to do so I must seem indifferent, yet make his life so attractive that he will not command our departure."

"One would fancy life could not but be attractive to the prince in the gayest city of the world," I said, as the princess paused for breath.

"He cares little for the polished pleasures which delight a Parisian, and insists on bringing many of his favorite amusements with him. His caprices amuse the world, and are admired, but they annoy me much. At home he wears his Russian costume, orders the horrible dishes he loves, and makes the apartments unendurable with his samovar, chibouk and barbarous ornaments. Abroad he drives his droschky with the Ischvostchik in full St. Petersburg livery, and wears his uniform on all occasions. I say nothing, but I suffer."

It required a strong effort to repress a smile at the princess's pathetic lamentations and the martyr-like airs she assumed. She was infinitely amusing with her languid or vivacious words and attitudes; her girlish frankness and her feeble health interested me, and I resolved to stay even before she asked my decision.

I sat with her an hour, chatting of many things, and feeling more and more at ease as I read the shallow but amiable nature before me. All arrangements were made, and I was about taking my leave when the prince entered unannounced, and so quickly that I had not time to make my escape.

He had made his toilet since I saw him last, and I found it difficult to recognize the picturesque figure on the ottoman in the person who entered wearing the ordinary costume of a well-dressed gentleman. Even the face seemed changed, for a cold, haughty expression replaced the thoughtful look it had worn in repose. A smile softened it as he greeted his sister, but it vanished as he turned to me, with a slight inclination, when she whispered my name and errand, and while she explained he stood regarding me with a look that angered me. Not that it was insolent, but supremely masterful, as if those proud eyes were accustomed to command whomever they looked upon. It annoyed me, and I betrayed my annoyance by a rebellious glance, which made him lift his brows in surprise as a half smile passed over his lips. When his sister paused, he said, in the purest French, and with a slightly imperious accent:

"Mademoiselle is an Englishwoman?"

"My mother was English, my father of Russian parentage, although born in England."

I knew not by what title to address the questioner, so I simplified the matter by using none at all.

"Ah, you are half a Russian, then, and naturally desire to see your country?"

"Yes, I have long wished it," I began, but a soft cough from the princess reminded me that I must check my wish till it was safe to express it.

"We return soon, and it is well that you go willingly. Mademoiselle sets you a charming example, Nadja; I indulge the hope that you will follow it."

As he spoke the princess shot a quick glance at me, and answered, in a careless tone:

"I seldom disappoint your hopes, Alexis; but mademoiselle agrees with me that St. Petersburg at this season is unendurable."

"Has mademoiselle tried it?" was the quiet reply, as the prince fixed his keen eyes full upon me, as if suspecting a plot.

"Not yet, and I have no desire to do so—the report satisfies me," I answered, moving to go.

The prince shrugged his shoulders, touched his sister's cheek, bowed slightly, and left the room as suddenly as he had entered.

The princess chid me playfully for my *maladresse*, begged to see me on the morrow, and graciously dismissed me. As I waited in the great hall a moment for my carriage to drive round, I witnessed a little scene which made a curious impression on me. In a small anteroom, the door of which was ajar, stood the prince, drawing on his gloves, while the lad whom I had seen above was kneeling before him, fastening a pair of fur-lined overshoes. Something was amiss with one clasp, the prince seemed impatient, and after a sharp word in Russian, angrily lifted his foot with a gesture that sent the lad backward with painful violence. I involuntarily uttered an exclamation, the prince turned quickly, and our eyes met. Mine I know were full of indignation and disgust, for I resented the kick more than the poor lad, who, meekly gathering himself up, finished his task without a word, like one used to such rebukes.

The haughtiest surprise was visible in the face of the prince, but no shame; and as I moved away I heard a low laugh, as if my demonstration amused him.

"Laugh if you will, Monsieur le Prince, but remember all your servants are not serfs," I muttered, irefully, as I entered the carriage.

CHAPTER II

All went smoothly for a week or two, and I not only found my new home agreeable but altogether luxurious, for the princess had taken a fancy to me and desired to secure me by every means in her power, as she confided to Madame Bayard. I had been in a treadmill so long that any change would have been pleasant, but this life was as charming as anything but entire freedom could be. The very caprices of the princess were agreeable, for they varied what otherwise might have been somewhat monotonous, and her perfect simplicity and frankness soon did away with any shyness of mine. As madame said, rank was nothing after all, and in this case princess was but a name, for many an untitled Parisienne led a gayer and more splendid life than Nadja Tcherinski, shut up in her apartments and dependent upon those about her for happiness. Being younger than myself, and one of the clinging, confiding women who must lean on some one, I soon felt that protective fondness which one cannot help feeling for the weak, the sick, and the unhappy. We read English, embroidered, sung, talked, and drove out together, for the princess received little company and seldom joined the revels which went on in the other wing of the hotel.

The prince came daily to visit his sister, and she always exerted herself to make these brief interviews as agreeable as possible. I was pressed into the service, and sung, played, or talked as the princess signified—finding that, like most Russians of good birth, the prince was very accomplished, particularly in languages and music. But in spite of these gifts and the increasing affability of his manners toward myself, I always felt that under all the French polish was hidden the Tartar wildness, and often saw the savage in his eye while his lips were smiling blandly. I did not like him, but my vanity was gratified by the daily assurances of the princess that I possessed and exerted an unconscious influence over him. It was interesting to match him, and soon exciting to try my will against his in covert ways. I did not fear him as his sister did, because over me he had no control, and being of as proud a spirit as himself, I paid him only the respect due to his rank, not as an inferior, but an equal, for my family was good, and he lacked the real princeliness of nature which commands the reverence of the highest. I think he felt this instinctively, and it angered him; but he betrayed nothing of it in words, and was coolly courteous to the incomprehensible *dame-de-compagnie* of his sister.

My apartments were near the princess's, but I never went to her till summoned, as her hours of rising were uncertain. As I sat one day awaiting the call of Claudine, her maid came to me looking pale and terrified.

"Madame la Princesse waits, mademoiselle, and begs you will pardon this long delay."

"What agitates you?" I asked, for the girl glanced nervously over her shoulder as she spoke, and seemed eager, yet afraid to speak.

"Ah, mademoiselle, the prince has been with her, and so afflicted her, it desolates me to behold her. He is quite mad at times, I think, and terrifies us by his violence. Do not breathe to any one this that I say, and comfort madame if it is possible," and with her finger on her lips the girl hurried away.

I found the princess in tears, but the moment I appeared she dropped her handkerchief to exclaim with a gesture of despair: "We are lost! We are lost! Alexis is bent on returning to Russia and taking me to my death. *Chère* Sybil, what is to be done?"

"Refuse to go, and assert at once your freedom; it is a case which warrants such decision," was my revolutionary advice, though I well knew the princess would as soon think of firing the Tuileries as opposing her brother.

"It is impossible, I am dependent on him, he never would forgive such an act, and I should repent it to my last hour. No, my hope is in you, for you have eloquence, you see my feeble state, and you can plead for me as I cannot plead for myself."

"Dear madame, you deceive yourself. I have no eloquence, no power, and it is scarcely for me to come between you and the prince. I will do my best, but it will be in vain, I think."

"No, you do not fear him, he knows that, and it gives you power; you can talk well, can move and convince; I often see this when you read and converse with him, and I know that he would listen. Ah, for my sake make the attempt, and save me from that dreadful place!" cried the princess imploringly.

"Well, madame, tell me what passed, that I may know how to conduct the matter. Is a time for departure fixed?"

"No, thank heaven; if it were I should despair, for he would never revoke his orders. Something has annoyed him; I fancy a certain lady frowns upon him; but be that as it may, he is eager to be gone, and desired me to prepare to leave Paris. I implored, I wept, I reproached, and caressed, but nothing moved him, and he left me with the look which forebodes a storm."

"May I venture to ask why the prince does not return alone, and permit you to join him in the spring?"

"Because when my poor Feodor died he gave me into my brother's care, and Alexis swore to guard me as his life. I am so frail, so helpless, I need a faithful protector, and but for his fearful temper I should desire no better one than my brother. I owe everything to him, and would gladly obey even in this matter but for my health."

"Surely he thinks of that? He will not endanger your life for a selfish wish?"

"He thinks me fanciful, unreasonably fearful, and that I make this an excuse to have my own way. He is never ill, and knows nothing of my suffering, for I do not annoy him with complaints."

"Do you not think, madame, that if we could once convince him of the reality of the danger he would relent?"

"Perhaps; but how convince him? He will listen to no one."

"Permit me to prove that. If you will allow me to leave you for an hour I fancy I can find a way to convince and touch the prince."

The princess embraced me cordially, bade me go at once, and return soon, to satisfy her curiosity. Leaving her to rest and wonder, I went quietly away to the celebrated physician who at intervals visited the princess, and stating the case to him, begged for a written opinion which, coming from him, would, I knew, have weight with the prince. Dr. Segarde at once complied, and strongly urged the necessity of keeping the princess in Paris some months longer. Armed with this, I hastened back, hopeful and gay.

The day was fine, and wishing to keep my errand private, I had not used the carriage placed at my disposal. As I crossed one of the long corridors, on my way to the princess, I was arrested by howls of pain and the sharp crack of a whip, proceeding from an apartment near by. I paused involuntarily, longing yet fearing to enter and defend poor Mouche, for I recognized his voice. As I stood, the door swung open and the great hound sprang out, to cower behind me, with an imploring look in his almost human eyes. The prince followed, whip in hand, evidently in one of the fits of passion which terrified the household. I had seen many demonstrations of wrath, but never anything like that, for he seemed literally beside himself. Pale as death, with eyes full of savage fire, teeth set, and hair bristling like that of an enraged animal, he stood fiercely glaring at me. My heart fluttered for a moment, then was steady, and feeling no fear, I lifted my eyes to his, freely showing the pity I felt for such utter want of self-control.

It irritated him past endurance, and pointing to the dog, he said, in a sharp, low voice, with a gesture of command:

"Go on, mademoiselle, and leave Mouche to his fate."

"But what has the poor beast done to merit such brutal punishment?" I asked, coolly, remaining where I was.

"It is not for you to ask, but to obey," was the half-breathless answer, for a word of opposition increased his fury.

"Pardon; Mouche takes refuge with me; I cannot betray him to his enemy."

The words were still on my lips, when, with a step, the prince reached me, and towering above me like the incarnation of wrath, cried fiercely, as he lifted his hand menacingly:

"If you thwart me it will be at your peril!"

I saw he was on the point of losing all control of himself, and seizing the upraised arm, I looked him in the eye, saying steadily:

"Monsieur le Prince forgets that in France it is dastardly to strike a woman. Do not disgrace yourself by any Russian brutality."

The whip dropped from his hand, his arm fell, and turning suddenly, he dashed into the room behind him. I was about to make good my retreat, when a strange sound made me glance into the room. The prince had flung himself into a chair, and sat there actually choking with the violence of his passion. His face was purple, his lips pale, and his eyes fixed, as he struggled to unclasp the great sable-lined cloak he wore. As he then looked I was afraid he would have a fit, and never stopping for a second thought, I hurried to him, undid the cloak, loosened his collar, and filling a glass from the *carafe* on the sideboard, held it to his lips. He drank mechanically, sat motionless a moment, then drew a long breath, shivered as if recovering from a swoon, and glanced about him till his eye fell on me. It kindled again, and passing his hand over his forehead as if to collect himself, he said abruptly:

"Why are you here?"

"Because you needed help, and there was no one else to give it," I answered, refilling the glass, and offering it again, for his lips seemed dry.

He took it silently, and as he emptied it at a draught his eye glanced from the whip to me, and a scarlet flush rose to his forehead.

"Did I strike you?" he whispered, with a shame-stricken face.

"If you had we should not have been here."

"And why?" he asked, in quick surprise.

"I think I should have killed you, or myself, after such degradation. Unwomanly, perhaps, but I have a man's sense of honor."

It was an odd speech, but it rose to my lips, and I uttered it impulsively, for my spirit was roused by the insult. It served me better than tears or reproaches, for his eye fell after a furtive glance, in which admiration, shame and pride contended, and forcing a smile, he said, as if to hide his discomposure:

"I have insulted you; if you demand satisfaction I will give it, mademoiselle."

"I do," I said, promptly.

He looked curious, but seemed glad of anything which should divert his thoughts from himself, for with a bow and a half smile, he said quickly:

"Will mademoiselle name the reparation I shall make her? Is it to be pistols or swords?"

"It is pardon for poor Mouche."

His black brow lowered, and the thunderbolt veins on his forehead darkened again with the angry blood, not yet restored to quietude. It cost him an effort to say gravely:

"He has offended me, and cannot be pardoned yet; ask anything for yourself, mademoiselle."

I was bent on having my own way, and making him submit as a penance for his unwomanly menace. Once conquer his will, in no matter how slight a degree, and I had gained a power possessed by no other person. I liked the trial, and would not yield one jot of the advantage I had gained; so I answered, with a smile I had never worn to him before:

"Monsieur le Prince has given his word to grant me satisfaction; surely he will not break it, whatever atonement I demand! Ah, pardon Mouche, and I forget the rest."

I had fine eyes, and knew how to use them; as I spoke I fixed them on the prince with an expression half-imploring, half-commanding, and saw in his face a wish to yield, but pride would not permit it.

"Mademoiselle, I ordered the dog to follow me; he refused, and for that I would have punished him. If I relent before the chastisement is finished I lose my power over him, and the offense will be repeated. Is it not possible to satisfy you without ruining Mouche?"

"Permit one question before I reply. Did you give yourself the trouble of discovering the cause of the dog's unusual disobedience before the whip was used?"

"No; it is enough for me that the brute refused to follow. What cause could there have been for his rebelling?"

"Call him and it will appear."

The prince ordered in the dog; but in vain; Mouche crouched in the corridor with a forlorn air, and answered only by a whine. His master was about to go to him angrily, when, to prevent another scene, I called, and at once the dog came limping to my feet. Stooping, I lifted one paw, and showed the prince a deep and swollen wound, which explained the poor brute's unwillingness to follow his master on the long daily drive. I was surprised at the way in which the prince received the rebuke; I expected a laugh, a careless or a haughty speech, but like a boy he put his arm about the hound, saying almost tenderly:

"Pardon, pardon, my poor Mouche! Who has hurt thee so cruelly? Forgive the whip; thou shalt never feel it again."

Like a noble brute as he was, Mouche felt the change, understood, forgave, and returned to his allegiance at once, lifting himself to lick his master's hand and wag his tail in token of affection. It was a pretty little scene, for the prince laid his face on the smooth head of the dog, and half-whispered his regrets, exactly as a generous-hearted lad would have done to the favorite whom he had wronged in anger. I was glad to see it, childish as it was, for it satisfied me that this household tyrant had a heart, and well pleased with the ending of this stormy interview, I stole noiselessly away, carrying the broken whip with me as a trophy of my victory. . . .

I was intensely curious to see how the prince would behave when we met. Politeness is such a national trait in France, where the poorest workman lifts his cap in passing a lady, to the Emperor, who returns the salute of his shabbiest subject, that one soon learns to expect the little courtesies of daily life so scrupulously and gracefully paid by all classes, and to miss them if they are wanting. When he chose, the prince was a perfect Frenchman in this respect, but at times nothing could be more insolently haughty, or entirely oblivious of common civility. Hitherto I had had no personal experience of this, but had observed it toward others, and very unnecessarily angered myself about it. My turn came now; for when he entered his sister's apartment next day, he affected entire unconsciousness of my presence. Not a look, word, or gesture was vouchsafed me, but, half turning his back, he chatted with the princess in an unusually gay and affectionate manner.

After the first indignant impulse to leave the room had passed, I became cool enough to see and enjoy the ludicrous side of the affair. I could not help wondering if it was done for effect, but for the first time since I came I saw the prince in his uniform. I would not look openly, though I longed to do so, for covert glances, as I busied myself with my embroidery, gave me glimpses of a splendid blending of scarlet, white and gold. It would have been impossible for the prince not to have known that this brilliant costume was excessively becoming, and not to have felt a very natural desire to display his handsome figure to advantage. More than once he crossed the room to look from the window, as if impatient for the droschky, then sat himself down at the piano and played stormily for five minutes, marched back to the princess's sofa and teased Bijou the poodle, ending at length by standing erect on the rug and facing the enemy.

Finding I bore my disgrace with equanimity, he was possessed to play the master, and show his displeasure in words as well as by silence. Turning to his sister, he said, in the tone of one who does not deign to issue commands to inferiors:

"You were enjoying some book as I entered, Nadja; desire Mademoiselle Varna to continue—I go in a moment."

"*Ma chère,* oblige me by finishing the chapter," said the princess, with a significant glance, and I obeyed.

We were reading George Sand's *Consuelo,* or rather the sequel of that wonderful book, and had reached the scenes in which Frederick the Great torments the prima donna before sending her to prison, because she will not submit to his whims. I liked my task, and read with spirit, hoping the prince would enjoy the lesson as much as I did. By skillfully cutting paragraphs here and there, I managed to get in the most apposite and striking of Consuelo's brave and sensible remarks, as well as the tyrant's unjust and ungenerous commands. The prince stood with his eyes fixed upon me. I felt, rather than saw this, for I never lifted my own, but permitted a smile to appear when Frederick threatened her with his cane. The princess speedily forgot everything but the romance, and when I paused, exclaimed, with a laugh:

"Ah, you enjoy that much, Sybil, for, like Consuelo, you would have defied the Great Fritz himself."

"That I would, in spite of a dozen Spondous. Royalty and rank give no one a right to oppress others. A tyrant—even a crowned one—is the most despicable of creatures," I answered, warmly.

"But you will allow that Porporina was very cold and coy, and altogether provoking, in spite of her genius and virtue," said the princess, avoiding the word "tyrant," as the subjects of the czar have a tendency to do.

"She was right, for the humblest mortals should possess their liberty and preserve it at all costs. Golden chains are often heavier than iron ones: is it not so, Mouche?" I asked of the dog, who lay at my feet, vainly trying to rid himself of the new collar which annoyed him.

A sharp "Here, sir!" made him spring to his master, who ordered him to lie down, and put one foot on him to keep him, as he showed signs of deserting again. The prince looked ireful, his black eyes were kindling, and some imperious speech was trembling on his lips, when Claudine entered with the *mal-apropos* question.

"Does Madame la Princesse desire that I begin to make preparations for the journey?"

"Not yet. Go; I will give orders when it is time," replied the princess, giving me a glance, which said, "We must speak now."

"What journey?" demanded the prince, as Claudine vanished precipitately.

"That for which you commanded me to prepare," returned his sister, with a heavy sigh.

"That is well. You consent, then, without more useless delay?" and the prince's face cleared as he spoke.

"If you still desire it, after reading this, I shall submit, Alexis," and giving him the note, his sister waited, with nervous anxiety, for his decision.

As he read I watched him, and saw real concern, surprise, and regret in his face, but when he looked up, it was to ask:

"When did Dr. Segarde give you this, and wherefore?"

"You shall know all, my brother. Mademoiselle sees my sufferings, pities my unhappiness, and is convinced that it is no whim of mine which makes me dread this return. I implore her to say this to you, to plead for me, because, with all your love, you cannot know my state as she does. To this prayer of mine she listens, but with a modesty as great as her goodness, she fears that you may think her officious, over-bold, or blinded by regard for me.

"Therefore she wisely asks for Segarde's opinion, sure that it will touch and influence you. Do not destroy her good opinion, nor disappoint thy Nadja!"

The prince *was* touched, but found it hard to yield, and said, slowly, as he refolded the note, with a glance at me of annoyance not anger:

"So you plot and intrigue against me, ladies! But I have said we shall go, and I never revoke a decree."

"Go!" cried the princess, in a tone of despair.

"Yes, it is inevitable," was the answer, as the prince turned toward the fire, as if to escape importunities and reproaches.

"But when, Alexis—when? Give me still a few weeks of grace!" implored his sister, approaching him in much agitation.

"I give thee till April," replied the prince, in an altered tone.

"But that is spring, the time I pray for! Do you, then, grant my prayer?" exclaimed the princess, pausing in amazement.

"I said we must go, but not *when;* now I fix a time, and give thee yet some weeks of grace. Didst thou think I loved my own pleasure more than thy life, my sister?"

As he turned, with a smile of tender reproach, the princess uttered a cry of joy and threw herself into his arms in a paroxysm of gratitude, delight and affection. I never imagined that the prince could unbend so beautifully and entirely; but as I watched him caress and reassure the frail creature who clung to him, I was surprised to find what a hearty admiration suddenly sprung up within me for "the barbarian," as I often called him to myself. I enjoyed the pretty tableau a moment, and was quietly gliding away, lest I should be *de trop*, when the princess arrested me by exclaiming, as she leaned on her brother's arm, showing a face rosy with satisfaction:

"*Chère* Sybil, come and thank him for this kindness; you know how ardently I desired the boon, and you must help me to express my gratitude."

"In what language shall I thank Monsieur le Prince for prolonging his sister's life? Your tears, madame, are more eloquent than any words of mine," I replied, veiling the reproach under a tone of respectful meekness.

"She is too proud, this English Consuelo; she will not stoop to confess an obligation even to Alexis Demidoff."

He spoke in a half-playful, half-petulant tone, and hesitated over the last words, as if he would have said "a prince." The haughtiness was quite gone, and something in his expression, attitude and tone touched me. The sacrifice had cost him something, and a little commendation would not hurt him, vain and selfish though he might be. I was grateful for the poor princess's sake, and I did not hesitate to show it, saying with my most cordial smile, and doubtless some of the satisfaction I could not but feel visible in my face:

"I am not too proud to thank you sincerely for this favor to Madame la Princesse, nor to ask pardon for anything by which I may have offended you."

A gratified smile rewarded me as he said, with an air of surprise:

"And yet, mademoiselle desires much to see St. Petersburg?"

"I do, but I can wait, remembering that it is more blessed to give than to receive."

A low bow was the only reply he made, and with a silent caress to his sister he left the room.

"You have not yet seen the droschky; from the window of the ante-room the courtyard is visible; go, mademoiselle, and get a glimpse of St. Petersburg," said the princess, returning to her sofa, weary with the scene.

I went, and looking down, saw the most picturesque equipage I had ever seen. The elegant, coquettish droschky with a pair of splendid black Ukraine horses, harnessed in the Russian fashion, with a network of purple leather profusely ornamented with silver, stood before the grand entrance, and on the seat sat a handsome young man in full Ischvostchik costume. His caftan of fine cloth was slashed at the sides with embroidery; his hat had a velvet band, a silver buckle, and a bunch of rosy ribbons in it; a white-laced neckcloth, buckskin gloves, hair and beard in perfect order; a brilliant sash and a crimson silk shirt. As I stood wondering if he was a serf, the prince appeared, wrapped in the long gray capote, lined with scarlet, which all military Russians wear, and the brilliant helmet surmounted by a flowing white plume. As he seated himself among the costly furs he glanced up at his sister's windows, where she sometimes stood to see him. His quick eye recognized me, and to my surprise he waved his hand with a gracious smile as the fiery horses whirled him away.

That smile haunted me curiously all day, and more than once I glanced into the courtyard, hoping to see the picturesque droschky again, for, though one cannot live long in Paris without seeing nearly every costume under the sun, and accustomed as I was to such sights, there was something peculiarly charming to me in the martial figure, the brilliant equipage and the wild black horses, as full of untamed grace and power as if but just brought from the steppes of Tartary.

There was a dinner party in the evening, and, anxious to gratify her brother, the princess went down. Usually I enjoyed these free hours, and was never at a loss for occupation or amusement, but on this evening I could settle to nothing till I resolved to indulge an odd whim which possessed me. Arranging palette and brushes, I was soon absorbed in reproducing on a small canvas a likeness of the droschky and its owner. Hour after hour slipped by as the little picture grew, and horses, vehicle, driver and master took shape and color under my touch. I spent much time on the principal figure, but left the face till the last. All was carefully copied from memory, the white tunic, golden cuirass, massive epaulets, and silver sash; the splendid casque with its plume, the gray cloak, and the scarlet trowsers, half-hidden by the high boots of polished leather. At the boots I paused, trying to remember something.

"Did he wear spurs?" I said, half audibly, as I leaned back to survey my work complacently.

"Decidedly yes, mademoiselle," replied a voice, and there stood the prince with a wicked smile on his lips.

I seldom lose my self-possession, and after an involuntary start, was quite myself, though much annoyed at being discovered. Instead of hiding the picture or sitting dumb with embarrassment, I held it up, saying tranquilly:

"Is it not creditable to so bad an artist? I was in doubt about the spurs, but now I can soon finish."

"The horses are wonderful, and the furs perfect. Ivan is too handsome, and this countenance may be said to lack expression."

He pointed to the blank spot where his own face should have been, and eyed me with most exasperating intelligence. But I concealed my chagrin under an innocent air, and answered simply:

"Yes; I wait to find a portrait of the czar before I finish this addition to my little gallery of kings and queens."

"The czar!" ejaculated the prince, with such an astonished expression that I could not restrain a smile, as I touched up the handsome Ivan's beard.

"I have an admiration for the droschky, and that it may be quite complete, I boldly add the czar. It always pleased me to read how freely and fearlessly he rides among his people, unattended, in the gray cloak and helmet."

The prince gave me an odd look, crossed the room, and returning, laid before me an enameled casket, on the lid of which was a portrait of a stout, light-haired, somewhat ordinary, elderly gentleman, saying in a tone which betrayed some pique and much amusement:

"Mademoiselle need not wait to finish her work: behold the czar!"

I was strongly tempted to laugh, and own the truth, but something in the prince's manner restrained me, and after gravely regarding the portrait a moment, I began to copy it. My hand was not steady nor my eye clear, but I recklessly daubed on till the prince, who had stood watching me, said suddenly in a very mild tone:

"I flatter myself that there was some mistake last evening; either Mouche failed to do his errand, or the design of the trinket displeased you. I have endeavored to suit mademoiselle's taste better, and this time I offer it myself."

A white-gloved hand holding an open jewel-case which contained a glittering ring came before my eyes, and I could not retreat. Being stubborn by nature, and ruffled by what had just passed, as well as bent on having my own way in the matter, I instantly decided to refuse all gifts. Retreating slightly from the offering, I pointed to the flowers on the table near me, and said, with an air of grave decision:

"Monsieur le Prince must permit me to decline. I have already received all that it is possible to accept."

"Nay, examine the trifle, mademoiselle, and relent. Why will you not oblige me and be friends, like Mouche?" he said, earnestly.

That allusion to the dog nettled me, and I replied, coldly turning from the importunate hand.

"It was not the silver collar which consoled poor Mouche for the blows. Like him I can forgive, but I cannot so soon forget."

The dainty case closed with a sharp snap, and flinging it on to a table as he passed, the prince left the room without a word.

I was a little frightened at what I had done for a moment, but soon recovered my courage, resolving that since he had made it a test which should yield, *I* would not be the one to do it, for I had right on my side. Nor would I be appeased till he had made the *amende honorable* to me as to the dog. I laughed at the foolish affair, yet could not entirely banish a feeling of anger at the first violence and at the lordly way in which he tried to atone for the insult.

"Let us wait and see how the sultan carries himself to-morrow," I said; "if he become tyrannical, I am free to go, thank heaven; otherwise it is interesting to watch the handsome savage chafe and fret behind the bars of civilized society."

And gathering up my work, I retired to my room to replace the czar's face with that of the prince.

[In the omitted Chapters IV and V, Sybil hurts her ankle and faints. She wakes from unconsciousness to find that her "bonnet and gloves were off. . . . Who had removed them? My hair was damp with eau-de-cologne; who had bathed my head? My injured foot lay on a cushion; who placed it there? Did I dream that a tender voice exclaimed, 'My little Sybil, my heart, speak to me'? or did the prince really utter such words?" The sexual duel continues, and Sybil acknowledges that she likes "courage in love as in war" and respects "a man who conquers all obstacles."]

CHAPTER VI

The next day we set out, but the dreaded journey proved delightful, for the weather was fine, and the prince in a charming mood. No allusion was made to the unexpected delay, except by the princess, who privately expressed her wonder at my power, and treated me with redoubled confidence and affection. We loitered by the way, and did not reach St. Petersburg till June.

I had expected changes in my life as well as change of scene, but was unprepared for the position which it soon became evident I was to assume. In Paris I had been the companion, now I was treated as a friend and equal by both the prince and princess. They entirely ignored my post, and remembering only that I was by birth a gentlewoman, by a thousand friendly acts made it impossible for me to refuse the relations which they chose to establish between us. I suspect the princess hinted to her intimates that I was a connection of her own, and my name gave color to the statement. Thus I found myself received with respect and interest by the circle in which I now moved, and truly enjoyed the free, gay life, which seemed doubly charming, after years of drudgery.

With this exception there was less alteration in my surroundings than I had imagined, for the upper classes in Russia speak nothing but French; in dress, amusements, and manners, copy French models so carefully that I should often have fancied myself in Paris, but for the glimpses of barbarism, which observing eyes cannot fail to detect, in spite of the splendor which surrounds them. The hotel of the prince was a dream of luxury; his equipages magnificent; his wealth apparently boundless; his friends among the highest in the land. He appeared to unusual advantage at home, and seemed anxious that I should observe this, exerting himself in many ways to impress me with his power, even while he was most affable and devoted.

I could no longer blind myself to the truth, and tried to meet it honestly. The prince loved me, and made no secret of his preference, though not a word had passed his lips. I had felt this since the night he carried me in his arms, but remembering the difference in rank, had taught myself to see in it only the passing caprice of a master for a servant, and as such, to regard it as an insult. Since we came to St. Petersburg the change in his manner seemed to assure me that he sought me as an equal, and desired to do me honor in the eyes of those about us. This soothed my pride and touched my heart, but, alluring as the thought was to my vanity and my ambition, I did not yield to it, feeling that I should not love, and that such an alliance was not the one for me.

Having come to this conclusion, I resolved to abide by it, and did so the more inflexibly as the temptation to falter grew stronger. My calm, cool manner perplexed and irritated the prince, who seemed to grow more passionate as test after test failed to extort any betrayal of regard from me. The princess, absorbed in her own affairs, seemed apparently blind to her brother's infatuation, till I was forced to enlighten her.

July was nearly over, when the prince announced that he was about to visit one of his estates, some versts from the city, and we were to accompany him. I had discovered that Volnoi was a solitary place, that no guests were expected, and that the prince was supreme master of everything and everybody on the estate. This did not suit me, for Madame Yermaloff, an Englishwoman, who had conceived a friendship for me, had filled my head with stories of Russian barbarity, and the entire helplessness of whomsoever dared to thwart or defy a Russian seigneur, especially when on his own domain. I laughed at her gossip, yet it influenced my decision, for of late the prince had looked ireful, and his black eyes had kept vigilant watch over me. I knew that his patience was exhausted, and feared that a stormy scene was in store for me. To avoid all further annoyance, I boldly stated the case to the princess, and decidedly refused to leave St. Petersburg.

To my surprise, she agreed with me; and I discovered, what I had before suspected, that, much as she liked me as a friend, the princess would have preferred her brother to marry one of his own rank. She delicately hinted this, yet, unwilling to give me up entirely, begged me to remain with Madame Yermaloff till she returned, when some new arrangement might be made. I consented, and feeling unequal to a scene with the prince, left his sister to inform him of my decision, and went quietly to my friend, who gladly received me. Next morning the following note from the princess somewhat reassured me:

> MA CHERE SYBIL—We leave in an hour. Alexis received the news of your flight in a singular manner. I expected to see him half frantic; but no, he smiled, and said, tranquilly: "She fears and flies me; it is a sign of weakness, for which I thank her." I do not understand him; but when we are quiet at Volnoi, I hope to convince him that you are, as always, wise and prudent. Adieu! I embrace you tenderly.
>
> N.T.

A curious sense of disappointment and uneasiness took possession of me on reading this note, and, womanlike, I began to long for that which I had denied myself. Madame Yermaloff found me a very dull companion, and began to rally me on my preoccupation. I tried to forget, but could not, and often stole out to walk past the prince's hotel, now closed and silent. A week dragged slowly by, and I had begun to think the prince had indeed forgotten me, when I was convinced that he had not in a somewhat alarming manner. Returning one evening from a lonely walk in the Place Michel, with its green English square, I observed a carriage standing near the Palace Galitzin, and listlessly wondered who was about to travel, for the coachman was in his place and a servant stood holding the door open. As I passed I glanced in, but saw nothing, for in the act sudden darkness fell upon me; a cloak was dexterously thrown over me, enveloping my head and arms, and rendering me helpless. Some one lifted me into the carriage, the door closed, and I was driven rapidly away, in spite of my stifled cries and fruitless struggles. At first I was frantic with anger and fear, and rebelled desperately against the strong hold which restrained me. Not a word was spoken, but I felt sure, after the first alarm, that the prince was near me, and this discovery, though it increased my anger, allayed my fear. Being half-suffocated, I suddenly feigned faintness, and lay motionless, as if spent. A careful hand withdrew the thick folds, and as I opened my eyes they met those of the prince fixed on me, full of mingled solicitude and triumph.

"You! Yes; I might have known no one else would dare perpetrate such an outrage!" I cried, breathlessly, and in a tone of intense scorn, though my heart leaped with joy to see him.

He laughed, while his eyes flashed, as he answered, gayly:

"Mademoiselle forgets that she once said she 'liked courage in love as in war, and respected a man who conquered all obstacles.' I remember this, and, when other means fail dare to brave even her anger to gain my object."

"What is that object?" I demanded, as my eyes fell before the ardent glance fixed on me.

"It is to see you at Volnoi, in spite of your cruel refusal."

"I will not go."

And with a sudden gesture I dashed my hand through the window and cried for help with all my strength. In an instant I was pinioned again, and my cries stifled by the cloak, as the prince said, sternly:

"If mademoiselle resists, it will be the worse for her. Submit, and no harm will befall you. Accept the society of one who adores you, and permit yourself to be conquered by one who never yields— except to you," he added, softly, as he held me closer, and put by the cloak again.

"Let me go—I will be quiet," I panted, feeling that it was indeed idle to resist now, yet resolving that he should suffer for this freak.

"You promise to submit—to smile again, and be your charming self?" he said, in the soft tone that was so hard to deny.

"I promise nothing but to be quiet. Release me instantly!" and I tried to undo the clasp of the hand that held me.

"Not till you forgive me and look kind. Nay, struggle if you will, I like it, for till now you have been the master. See, I pardon all your cruelty, and find you more lovely than ever."

As he spoke he bent and kissed me on forehead, lips and cheek with an ardor which wholly daunted me. I did pardon him, for there was real love in his face, and love robbed the act of rudeness in my eyes, for instead of any show of anger or disdain, I hid my face in my hands, weeping the first tears he had ever seen me shed. It tamed him in a moment, for as I sobbed I heard him imploring me to be calm, promising to sin no more, and assuring me that he meant only to carry me to Volnoi as its mistress, whom he loved and honored above all women. Would I forgive his wild act, and let his obedience in all things else atone for this?

I must forgive it; and if he did not mock me by idle offers of obedience, I desired him to release me entirely and leave me to compose myself, if possible.

He instantly withdrew his arm, and seated himself opposite me, looking half contrite, half exultant, as he arranged the cloak about my feet. I shrunk into the corner and dried my tears, feeling unusually weak and womanish, just when I most desired to be strong and stern. Before I could whet my tongue for some rebuke, the prince uttered an exclamation of alarm, and caught my hand. I looked, and saw that it was bleeding from a wound made by the shattered glass.

"Let it bleed," I said, trying to withdraw it. But he held it fast, binding it up with his own handkerchief in the tenderest manner, saying as he finished, with a passionate pressure:

"Give it to me, Sybil, I want it—this little hand—so resolute, yet soft. Let it be mine, and it shall never know labor or wound again. Why do you frown—what parts us?"

"This," and I pointed to the crest embroidered on the corner of the *mouchoir*.

"Is that all?" he asked, bending forward with a keen glance that seemed to read my heart.

"One other trifle," I replied sharply.

"Name it, my princess, and I will annihilate it, as all other obstacles," he said, with the lordly air that became him.

"It is impossible."

"Nothing is impossible to Alexis Demidoff."

"I do not love you."

"In truth, Sybil?" he cried incredulously.

"In truth," I answered steadily.

He eyed me an instant with a gloomy air, then drew a long breath, and set his teeth, exclaiming:

"You are mortal. I shall *make* you love me."

"How, monsieur?" I coldly asked, while my traitorous heart beat fast.

"I shall humble myself before you, shall obey your commands, shall serve you, protect you, love and honor you ardently, faithfully, while I live. Will not such devotion win you?"

"No."

It was a hard word to utter, but I spoke it, looking him full in the eye and seeing with a pang how pale he grew with real despair.

"Is it because you love already, or that you have no heart?" he said slowly.

"I love already." The words escaped me against my will, for the truth would find vent in spite of me. He took it as I meant he should, for his lips whitened, as he asked hoarsely:

"And this man whom you love, is he alive?"

"Yes."

"He knows of this happiness—he returns your love?"

"He loves me; ask no more; I am ill and weary."

A gloomy silence reigned for several minutes, for the prince seemed buried in a bitter reverie, and I was intent on watching him. An involuntary sigh broke from me as I saw the shadow deepen on the handsome face opposite, and thought that my falsehood had changed the color of a life. He looked up at the sound, saw my white, anxious face, and without a word drew from a pocket of the carriage a flask and silver cup, poured me a draught of wine, and offered it, saying gently:

"Am I cruel in my love, Sybil?"

I made no answer, but drank the wine, and asked as I returned the cup:

"Now that you know the truth, must I go to Volnoi? Be kind, and let me return to Madame Yermaloff."

His face darkened and his eyes grew fierce, as he replied, with an aspect of indomitable resolve:

"It is impossible; I have sworn to make you love me, and at Volnoi I will work the miracle. Do you think this knowledge of the truth will deter me? No; I shall teach you to forget this man, whoever he is, and make you happy in my love. You doubt this. Wait a little and see what a real passion can do."

This lover-like pertinacity was dangerous, for it flattered my woman's nature more than any submission could have done. I dared not listen to it, and preferring to see him angry rather than tender, I said provokingly:

"No man ever forced a woman to love him against her will. You will certainly fail, for no one in her senses would give her heart to *you!*"

"And why? Am I hideous?" he asked, with a haughty smile.

"Far from it."

"Am I a fool, mademoiselle?"

"Quite the reverse."

"Am I base?"

"No."

"Have I degraded my name and rank by any act?"

"Never, till to-night, I believe."

He laughed, yet looked uneasy, and demanded imperiously:

"Then, why will no woman love me?"

"Because you have the will of a tyrant, and the temper of a madman."

If I had struck him in the face it would not have startled him as my blunt words did. He flushed scarlet, drew back and regarded me with a half-bewildered air, for never had such a speech been made to him before. Seeing my success, I followed it up by saying gravely:

"The insult of to-night gives me the right to forget the respect I have hitherto paid you, and for once you shall hear the truth as plain as words can make it. Many fear you for these faults, but no one dares tell you of them, and they mar an otherwise fine nature."

I got no further, for to my surprise, the prince said suddenly, with real dignity, though his voice was less firm than before:

"One dares to tell me of them, and I thank her. Will she add to the obligation by teaching me to cure them?" Then he broke out impetuously: "Sybil, you can help me; you possess courage and power to tame my wild temper, my headstrong will. In heaven's name I ask you to do it, that I may be worthy some good woman's love."

He stretched his hands toward me with a gesture full of force and feeling, and his eloquent eyes pleaded for pity. I felt my resolution melting away, and fortified myself by a chilly speech.

"Monsieur le Prince has said that nothing is impossible to him; if he can conquer all obstacles, it were well to begin with these."

"I have begun. Since I knew you my despotic will has bent more than once to yours, and my mad temper has been curbed by the remembrance that you have seen it. Sybil, if I do conquer myself, can you, will you try to love me?"

So earnestly he looked, so humbly he spoke, it was impossible to resist the charm of this new and manlier mood. I gave him my hand, and said, with the smile that always won him:

"I will respect you sincerely, and be your friend; more I cannot promise."

He kissed my hand with a wistful glance, and sighed as he dropped it, saying in a tone of mingled hope and resignation:

"Thanks; respect and friendship from you are dearer than love and confidence from another woman. I know and deplore the faults fostered by education and indulgence, and I will conquer them. Give me time. I swear it will be done."

"I believe it, and I pray for your success."

He averted his face and sat silent for many minutes, as if struggling with some emotion which he was too proud to show. I watched him, conscious of a redoubled interest in this man, who at one moment ruled me like a despot, and at another confessed his faults like a repentant boy.

CHAPTER VII

In Russia, from the middle of May to the 1st of August, there is no night. It is daylight till eleven, then comes a soft semi-twilight till one, when the sun rises. Through this gathering twilight we drove toward Volnoi. The prince let down the windows, and the summer air blew in refreshingly; the peace of the night soothed my perturbed spirit, and the long silences were fitly broken by some tender word from my companion, who, without approaching nearer, never ceased to regard me with eyes so full of love that, for the first time in my life, I dared not meet them.

It was near midnight when the carriage stopped, and I could discover nothing but a tall white pile in a wilderness of blooming shrubs and trees. Lights shone from many windows, and as the prince led me into a brilliantly lighted *salon,* the princess came smiling to greet me, exclaiming, as she embraced me with affection:

"Welcome, my sister. You see it is in vain to oppose Alexis. We must confess this, and yield gracefully; in truth, I am glad to keep you, *chère amie,* for without you we find life very dull."

"Madame mistakes; I never yield, and am here against my will."

I withdrew myself from her as I spoke, feeling hurt that she had not warned me of her brother's design. They exchanged a few words as I sat apart, trying to look dignified, but dying with sleep. The princess soon came to me, and it was impossible to resist her caressing manner as she begged me to go and rest, leaving all disagreements till the morrow. I submitted, and, with a silent salute to the prince, followed her to an apartment next her own, where I was soon asleep, lulled by the happy thought that I was not forgotten.

The princess was with me early in the morning, and a few moments' conversation proved to me that, so far from her convincing her brother of the folly of his choice, he had entirely won her to his side, and enlisted her sympathies for himself. She pleaded his suit with sisterly skill and eloquence, but I would pledge myself to nothing, feeling a perverse desire to be hardly won, if won at all, and a feminine wish to see my haughty lover thoroughly subdued before I put my happiness into his keeping. I consented to remain for a time, and a servant was sent to Madame Yermaloff with a letter explaining my flight, and telling where to forward a portion of my wardrobe.

Professing herself satisfied for the present, and hopeful for the future, the princess left me to join her brother in the garden, where I saw them talking long and earnestly. It was pleasant to a lonely soul like myself to be so loved and cherished, and when I descended it was impossible to preserve the cold demeanor I had assumed, for all faces greeted me with smiles, all voices welcomed me, and one presence made the strange place seem like home. The prince's behavior was perfect, respectful, devoted and self-controlled; he appeared like a new being, and the whole household seemed to rejoice in the change.

Day after day glided happily away, for Volnoi was a lovely spot, and I saw nothing of the misery hidden in the hearts and homes of the hundred serfs who made the broad domain so beautiful. I seldom saw them, never spoke to them, for I knew no Russ, and in our drives the dull-looking peasantry possessed no interest for me. They never came to the house, and the prince appeared to know nothing of them beyond what his Stavosta, or steward reported. Poor Alexis! he had many hard lessons to learn that year, yet was a better man and master for them all, even the one which nearly cost him his life.

Passing through the hall one day, I came upon a group of servants lingering near the door of the apartment in which the prince gave his orders and transacted business. I observed that the French servants looked alarmed, the Russian ones fierce and threatening, and that Antoine, the valet of the prince, seemed to be eagerly dissuading several of the serfs from entering. As I appeared he exclaimed:

"Hold, he is saved! Mademoiselle will speak for him; she fears nothing, and she pities every one." Then, turning to me, he added, rapidly: "Mademoiselle will pardon us that we implore this favor of her great kindness. Ivan, through some carelessness, has permitted the favorite horse of the prince to injure himself fatally. He has gone in to confess, and we fear for his life, because Monsieur le Prince loved the fine beast well, and will be in a fury at the loss. He killed poor Androvitch for a less offense, and we tremble for Ivan. Will mademoiselle intercede for him? I fear harm to my master if Ivan suffers, for these fellows swear to avenge him."

Without a word I opened the door and entered quietly. Ivan was on his knees, evidently awaiting his doom with dogged submission.

A pair of pistols lay on the table, and near it stood the prince, with the dark flush on his face, the terrible fire in his eyes which I had seen before. I saw there was no time to lose, and going to him, looked up into that wrathful countenance, whispering in a warning tone:

"Remember poor Androvitch."

It was like an electric shock; he started, shuddered, and turned pale; covered his face a moment and stood silent, while I saw drops gather on his forehead and his hand clinch itself spasmodically. Suddenly he moved, flung the pistols through the open window, and turning on Ivan, said, with a forceful gesture:

"Go. I pardon you."

The man remained motionless as if bewildered, till I touched him, bidding him thank his master and begone.

"No, it is you I thank, good angel of the house," he muttered, and lifting a fold of my dress to his lips Ivan hurried from the room.

I looked at the prince; he was gravely watching us, but a smile touched his lips as he echoed the man's last words, " 'Good angel of the house'; yes, in truth you are. Ivan is right, he owes me no thanks; and yet it was the hardest thing I ever did to forgive him the loss of my noble Sophron."

"But you did forgive him, and whether he is grateful or not, the victory is yours. A few such victories and the devil is cast out forever."

He seized my hand, exclaiming in a tone of eager delight:

"You believe this? You have faith in me, and rejoice that I conquer this cursed temper, this despotic will?"

"I do; but I still doubt the subjection of the will," I began; he interrupted me by an impetuous—

"Try it; ask anything of me and I will submit."

"Then let me return to St. Petersburg at once, and do not ask to follow."

He had not expected this, it was too much; he hesitated, demanding, anxiously:

"Do you really mean it?"

"Yes."

"You wish to leave me, to banish me now when you are all in all to me?"

"I wish to be free. You have promised to obey; yield your will to mine and let me go."

He turned and walked rapidly through the room, paused a moment at the further end, and coming back, showed me such an altered face that my conscience smote me for the cruel test. He looked at me in silence for an instant, but I showed no sign of relenting, although I saw what few had ever seen, those proud eyes wet with tears. Bending, he passionately kissed my hands, saying, in a broken voice:

"Go, Sybil. I submit."

"Adieu, my friend; I shall not forget," and without venturing another look I left him.

I had hardly reached my chamber and resolved to end the struggle for both of us, when I saw the prince gallop out of the courtyard like one trying to escape from some unfortunate remembrance or care.

"Return soon to me," I cried; "the last test is over and the victory won."

Alas, how little did I foresee what would happen before that return; how little did he dream of the dangers that encompassed him.

A tap at my door roused me as I sat in the twilight an hour later, and Claudine crept in, so pale and agitated that I started up, fearing some mishap to the princess.

"No, she is well and safe, but oh, mademoiselle, a fearful peril hangs over us all. Hush! I will tell you. I have discovered it, and we must save them."

"Save who? what peril? speak quickly."

"Mademoiselle knows that the people on the estate are poor ignorant brutes who hate the Stavosta, and have no way of reaching the prince except through him. He is a hard man; he oppresses them, taxes them heavily unknown to the prince, and they believe my master to be a tyrant. They have borne much, for when we are away the Stavosta rules here, and they suffer frightfully. I have lived long in Russia, and I hear many things whispered that do not reach the ears of my lady. These poor creatures bear long, but at last they rebel, and some fearful affair occurs, as at Bagatai, where the count-ess, a cruel woman, was one night seized by her serfs, who burned and tortured her to death."

"Good heavens! Claudine, what is this danger which menaces us?"

"I understand Russ, mademoiselle, have quick eyes and ears, and for some days I perceive that all is not well among the people. Ivan is changed; all look dark and threatening but old Vacil. I watch and listen, and discover that they mean to attack the house and murder the prince."

"*Mon Dieu!* but when?"

"I knew not till to-day. Ivan came to me and said, 'Mademoiselle Varna has saved my life. I am grateful. I wish to serve her. She came here against her will; she desires to go; the prince is away; I will pro-vide a horse to-night at dusk, and she can join her friend Madame Yermaloff, who is at Baron Narod's, only a verst distant. Say this to mademoiselle, and if she agrees, drop a signal from her window. I shall see and understand.' "

"But why think that the attack is to be to-night?"

"Because Ivan was so anxious to remove you. He urged me to persuade you, for the prince is gone, and the moment is propitious. You will go, mademoiselle?"

"No; I shall not leave the princess."

"But you can save us all by going, for at the baron's you can pro-cure help and return to defend us before these savages arrive. Ivan will believe you safe, and you can thwart their plans before the hour comes. Oh, mademoiselle, I conjure you to do this, for we are watched, and you alone will be permitted to escape."

A moment's thought convinced me that this was the only means of help in our power, and my plans were quickly laid. It was useless to wait for the prince, as his return was uncertain; it was unwise to alarm the princess, as she would betray all; the quick-witted Clau-dine and myself must do the work, and trust to heaven for success. I dropped a handkerchief from my window; a tall figure emerged from the shrubbery, and vanished, whispering:

"In an hour—at the chapel gate."

At the appointed time I was on the spot, and found Ivan holding the well-trained horse I often rode. It was nearly dark—for August brought night—and it was well for me, as my pale face would have betrayed me.

"Mademoiselle has not fear? If she dares not go alone I will guard her," said Ivan, as he mounted me.

"Thanks. I fear nothing. I have a pistol, and it is not far. Liberty is sweet. I will venture much for it."

"I also," muttered Ivan.

He gave me directions as to my route, and watched me ride away, little suspecting my errand.

How I rode that night! My blood tingles again as I recall the wild gallop along the lonely road, the excitement of the hour, and the resolve to save Alexis or die in the attempt. Fortunately I found a large party at the baron's, and electrified them by appearing in their midst, disheveled, breathless and eager with my tale of danger. What passed I scarcely remember, for all was confusion and alarm. I refused to remain, and soon found myself dashing homeward, followed by a gallant troop of five and twenty gentlemen. More time had been lost than I knew, and my heart sunk as a dull glare shone from the direction of Volnoi as we strained up the last hill.

Reaching the top, we saw that one wing was already on fire, and distinguished a black, heaving mass on the lawn by the flickering torchlight. With a shout of wrath the gentlemen spurred to the rescue, but I reached the chapel gate unseen, and entering, flew to find my friends. Claudine saw me and led me to the great saloon, for the lower part of the house was barricaded. Here I found the princess quite insensible, guarded by a flock of terrified French servants, and Antoine and old Vacil endeavoring to screen the prince, who, with reckless courage, exposed himself to the missiles which came crashing against the windows. A red light filled the room, and from without arose a yell from the infuriated mob more terrible than any wild beast's howl.

As I sprang in, crying, "They are here—the baron and his friends—you are safe!" all turned toward me as if every other hope was lost. A sudden lull without, broken by the clash of arms, verified my words, and with one accord we uttered a cry of gratitude. The prince flung up the window to welcome our deliverers; the red glare of the fire made him distinctly visible, and as he leaned out with a ringing shout, a hoarse voice cried menacingly:

"Remember poor Androvitch."

It was Ivan's voice, and as it echoed my words there was the sharp crack of a pistol, and the prince staggered back, exclaiming faintly:

"I forgive him; it is just."

We caught him in our arms, and as Antoine laid him down he looked at me with a world of love and gratitude in those magnificent eyes of his, whispering as the light died out of them:

"Always our good angel. Adieu, Sybil. I submit."

How the night went after that I neither knew nor cared, for my only thought was how to keep life in my lover till help could come. I learned afterward that the sight of such an unexpected force caused a panic among the serfs, who fled or surrendered at once. The fire was extinguished, the poor princess conveyed to bed, and the con-querors departed, leaving a guard behind. Among the gentlemen there fortunately chanced to be a surgeon, who extracted the ball from the prince's side.

I would yield my place to no one, though the baron implored me to spare myself the anguish of the scene. I remained steadfast, supporting the prince till all was over; then, feeling that my strength was beginning to give way, I whispered to the surgeon, that I might take a little comfort away with me:

"He will live? His wound is not fatal?"

The old man shook his head, and turned away, muttering regret-fully:

"There is no hope; say farewell, and let him go in peace, my poor child."

The room grew dark before me, but I had strength to draw the white face close to my own, and whisper tenderly:

"Alexis, I love you, and you alone. I confess my cruelty; oh, par-don me, before you die!"

A look, a smile full of the intensest love and joy, shone in the eyes that silently met mine as consciousness deserted me.

One month from that night I sat in that same saloon a happy woman, for on the couch, a shadow of his former self but alive and out of danger, lay the prince, my husband. The wound was not fatal, and love had worked a marvelous cure. While life and death still fought for him, I yielded to his prayer to become his wife, that he might leave me the protection of his name, the rich gift of his rank and fortune. In my remorse I would have granted anything, and when the danger was passed rejoiced that nothing could part us again.

As I sat beside him my eyes wandered from his tranquil face to the garden where the princess sat singing among the flowers, and then passed to the distant village where the wretched serfs drudged their lives away in ignorance and misery. They were mine now, and the weight of this new possession burdened my soul.

"I cannot bear it; this must be changed."

"It shall."

Unconsciously I had spoken aloud, and the prince had answered without asking to know my thoughts.

"What shall be done, Alexis?" I said, smiling, as I caressed the thin hand that lay in mine.

"Whatever you desire. I do not wait to learn the wish, I promise it shall be granted."

"Rash as ever; have you, then, no will of your own?"

"None; you have broken it."

"Good; hear then my wish. Liberate your serfs; it afflicts me as a free-born Englishwoman to own men and women. Let them serve you if they will, but not through force or fear. Can you grant this, my prince?"

"I do; the Stavosta is already gone, and they know I pardon them. What more, Sybil?"

"Come with me to England, that I may show my countrymen the brave barbarian I have tamed."

My eyes were full of happy tears, but the old tormenting spirit prompted the speech. Alexis frowned, then laughed, and answered, with a glimmer of his former imperious pride:

"I might boast that I also had tamed a fiery spirit, but I am humble, and content myself with the knowledge that the proudest woman ever born has promised to love, honor, and—"

"*Not* obey you," I broke in with a kiss.

"Woman's Part in the Concord Celebration"

(*Woman's Journal,* May 1, 1875)

L. M. ALCOTT

Being frequently asked "what part the women took in the Concord Centennial celebration?" I give herewith a brief account of our share on that occasion.

Having set our houses in order, stored our larders, and filled our rooms with guests, we girded up our weary souls and bodies for the great day, feeling that we must do or die for the honor of old Concord.

We had no place in the procession, but such women as wished to hear the oration were directed to meet in the town hall at half past nine, and there wait till certain persons, detailed for the service, should come to lead them to the tent, where a limited number of seats had been provided for the weaker vessels.

This seemed a sensible plan, and as a large proportion of ladies chose the intellectual part of the feast the hall was filled with a goodly crowd at the appointed hour. No one seemed to know what to do except wait, and that we did with the patience born of long practice. But it was very trying to the women of Concord to see invited guests wandering forlornly about or sitting in chilly corners meekly wondering why the hospitalities of the town were not extended to them as well as to their "men folks" who were absorbed into the pageant in one way or another.

For an hour we women waited, but no one came, and the sound of martial music so excited the patient party that with one accord we moved down to the steps below, where a glimpse of the approaching procession might cheer our eyes. Here we stood, with the north wind chilling us to the marrow of our bones, a flock of feminine Casabiancas with the slight difference of freezing instead of burning at our posts.

Some wise virgins, who put not their trust in men, departed to shift for themselves, but fifty or more obeyed orders and stood fast till, just as the procession appeared, an agitated gentleman with a rosette at his buttonhole gave the brief command,

"Ladies cross the common and wait for your escort:"

Then he vanished and was seen no more.

Over we went, like a flock of sheep, leaving the show behind us, but comforting ourselves with the thought of the seats "saving up" for us and of the treat to come. A cheerful crowd, in spite of the bitter wind, the rude comments of the men swarming by, and the sad certainty which slowly dawned upon us that we were entirely forgotten. The gay and gallant presence of a granddaughter of the Dr. Ripley who watched the fight from the Old Manse, kept up our spirits; for this indomitable lady circulated among us like sunshine, inspiring us with such confidence that we rallied round the little flag she bore, and followed where it led.

Patience has its limits, and there came a moment when the revolutionary spirit of '76 blazed up in the bosoms of these long suffering women; for, when some impetuous soul cried out "Come on and let us take care of ourselves!" there was a general movement; the flag fluttered to the front, veils were close reefed, skirts kilted up, arms locked, and with one accord the Light Brigade charged over the red bridge, up the hill, into the tented field, rosy and red-nosed, disheveled but dauntless.

The tent was closely packed, and no place appeared but a corner of the platform. Anxious to seat certain grey-haired ladies weary with long waiting, and emboldened by a smile from Senator Wilson, a nod from Representative May, and a pensive stare from Orator Curtis, I asked the President of the day if a few ladies could occupy that corner till seats could be found for them?

"They can sit or stand anywhere in the town except on this platform; and the quicker they get down the better, for gentlemen are coming in to take these places."

This gracious reply made me very glad to descend into the crowd again, for there at least good-nature reigned; and there we stood, placidly surveyed by the men (who occupied the seats set apart for us,) not one of whom stirred, though the grandmother of Boston waited in the ranks.

My idea of hospitality may be old-fashioned, but I must say I felt ashamed of Concord that day, when all I could offer my guests, admiring pilgrims to this "Mecca of the mind," was the extreme edge of an unplaned board; for, when the gods were settled, leave was given us to sit on the rim of the platform.

Perched there, like a flock of tempest tossed pigeons, we had the privilege of reposing among the sacred boots of the Gamalials at whose feet we sat, and of listening to the remarks of the reporters, who evidently felt that the elbow room of the almighty press should not be encroached upon even by a hair's breadth.

"No place for women," growled one.

"Never was a fitter," answered a strong-minded lady standing on one foot.

"Ought to have come earlier, if they come at all."

"So they would, if they had not obeyed orders. Never will again."

"Don't see why they couldn't be contented with seeing the procession."

"Because they preferred poetry and patriotism to fuss and feathers."

"Better have it all their own way, next time."

"No doubt they will, and I hope we shall all be there to see."

So the dialogue ended in a laugh, and the women resigned themselves to cold shoulders all around. But as I looked about me, it was impossible to help thinking that there should have been a place for the great granddaughters of Prescott, William Emerson, John Hancock and Dr. Ripley, as well as for Isaac Davis's old sword, the scissors that cut the immortal cartridges, and the ancient flag some woman's fingers made. It seemed to me that their presence on that platform would have had a deeper significance than the gold lace which adorned one side, or the senatorial ponderosity under which it broke down on the other; and that the men of Concord had missed a grand opportunity of imitating those whose memory they had met to honor.

The papers have told the tale of that day's exploits and experiences, but the papers did not get all the little items, and some of them were rather funny. Just before the services began, a distracted usher struggled in to inform Judge Hoar that the wives of several potentates had been left out in the cold, and must be accommodated. Great was the commotion then, for these ladies being bobs to political kites, could not be neglected; so a part of the seats reserved for women were with much difficulty cleared, and the "elect precious" set thereon. Dear ladies! how very cold and wretched they were when they got there, and how willingly the "free and independent citizenesses" of Concord forgave them for reducing their limited quarters to the point of suffocation, as they spread their cloaks over the velvet of their guests, still trying to be hospitable under difficulties.

When order was restored, what might be called "the Centennial Break Down" began. The President went first—was it an omen? and took refuge among the women, who I am happy to say received him kindly and tried to temper the wind to His Imperturbability, as he sat among them looking so bored that I longed to offer him a cigar.

The other gentleman stood by the ship, which greatly diversified the performances by slowly sinking with all on board but the captain. Even the orator tottered on the brink of ruin more than once, and his table would have gone over if a woman had not held up one leg of it for an hour or so. No light task, she told me afterward, for when the inspired gentleman gave an impressive thump, it took both hands to sustain the weight of his eloquence. Another lady was pinned down by the beams falling on her skirts, but cheerfully sacrificed them, and sat still, till the departure of the presidential party allowed us to set her free.

Finding us bound to hear it out, several weary gentlemen offered us their seats, after a time; but we had the laugh on our side now, and sweetly declined, telling them their platform was not strong enough to hold us.

It was over at last, and such of us as had strength enough left went to the dinner, and enjoyed another dish of patriotism "cold without;" others went home to dispense hot comforts, and thaw the congealed visitors who wandered to our doors.

Then came the ball, and there all went well, for Woman was in her sphere, her "only duty was to please," and the more there were, the merrier; so the deserted damsels of the morning found themselves the queens of the evening, and, forgetting and forgiving, bore their part as gaily as if they had put on the vigor of their grandmothers with the old brocades that became them so well.

Plenty of escorts, ushers and marshals at last, and six chairs apiece if we wanted them. Gentlemen who had been as grim as griffins a few hours before were all devotion now, and spectacles that had flashed awful lightning on the women who dared prefer poetry to polkas now beamed upon us benignly, and hoped we were enjoying ourselves, as we sat nodding along the walls while our guests danced.

That was the end of it, and by four A.M., peace fell upon the exhausted town, and from many a welcome pillow went up the grateful sigh:

"Thank heaven we shall not have to go through this again!"

No, not quite the end; for by and by there will come a day of reckoning, and then the tax-paying women of Concord will not be forgotten I think, will not be left to wait uncalled upon, or be considered in the way; and *then*, I devoutly wish that those who so bravely bore their share of that day's burden without its honor, will rally round their own flag again, and, following in the footsteps of their forefathers, will utter another protest that shall be "heard round the world."

LOUISA M. ALCOTT.

Concord, Mass.

8

Suffrage

William Henry Channing to the Woman's Rights Convention

(Rochester, N.Y., October 3, 1853)

To the President and Members of the Woman's Rights Convention:

As I am prevented, to my deep regret, from being present at the Convention, let me suggest in writing what I should prefer to speak. First, however, I would once again avow that I am with you heart, mind, soul, and strength for the Equal Rights of Women. This great reform will prove to be, I am well assured, the salvation and glory of this Republic, and of all Christian and civilized States:

> "And if at once we may not
> Declare the greatness of the work we plan,
> Be sure at least that ever in our eyes
> It stands complete before us as a dome
> Of light beyond this gloom—a house of stars
> Encompassing these dusky tents—a thing
> Near as our hearts, and perfect as the heavens.
> Be this our aim and model, and our hands
> Shall not wax faint, until the work is done."

The Woman's Rights Conventions, which, since 1848, have been so frequently held in New York, Ohio, Massachusetts, Pennsylvania, etc., have aroused respectful attention, and secured earnest sympathy, throughout the United States. It becomes the advocates of the Equal Rights of Women, then, to take advantage of this wide-spread interest and to press the Reform, at once, onward to practical results.

Among other timely measures, these have occurred to me as promising to be effective:

I. There should be prepared, printed, and widely circulated, A DECLARATION OF WOMAN'S RIGHTS.

This Declaration should distinctly announce the inalienable rights of women:

1st. As human beings,—irrespective of the distinction of sex— actively to co-operate in all movements for the elevation of mankind.

2d. As rational, moral, and responsible agents, freely to think, speak, and do, what truth and duty dictate, and to be the ultimate judges of their own sphere of action.

3d. As women, to exert in private and in public, throughout the whole range of Social Relations, that special influence which God assigns as their appropriate function, in endowing them with feminine attributes.

4th. As members of the body politic, needing the protection, liable to the penalties, and subject to the operation of the laws, to take their fair part in legislation and administration, and in appointing the makers and administrators of the laws.

5th. As constituting one-half of the people of these free and United States, and as nominally, free women, to possess and use the power of voting, now monopolized by that other half of the people, the free men.

6th. As property holders, numbered and registered in every census, and liable to the imposition of town, county, state, and national taxes, either to be represented if taxed, or to be left untaxed if unrepresented, according to the established precedent of No taxation without representation.

7th. As producers of wealth to be freed from all restrictions on their industry; to be remunerated according to the work done, and not the sex of the workers, and whether married or single, to be secured in the ownership of their gains, and the use and distribution of their property.

8th. As intelligent persons, to have ready access to the best means of culture, afforded by schools, colleges, professional institutions, museums of science, galleries of art, libraries, and reading-rooms.

9th. As members of Christian churches and congregations, heirs of Heaven and children of God, to preach the truth, to administer the rites of baptism, communion, and marriage, to dispense charities and in every way to quicken and refine the religious life of individuals and of society.

The mere announcement of these rights, is the strongest argument and appeal that can be made, in behalf of granting them. The claim to their free enjoyment is undeniably just. Plainly such rights are inalienable, and plainly too, woman is entitled to their possession equally with man. Our whole plan of government is a hypocritical farce, if one-half the people can be governed by the other half without their consent being asked or granted. Conscience and common sense alike demand the equal rights of women. To the conscience and common sense of their fellow-citizens, let women appeal untiringly, until their just claims are acknowledged throughout the whole system of legislation, and in all the usages of society.

And this introduces the next suggestion I have to offer.

II. Forms of petition should be drawn up and distributed for signatures, to be offered to the State Legislatures at their next sessions. These petitions should be directed to the following points:

1st. That the right of suffrage be granted to the people, universally, without distinction of sex; and that the age for attaining legal and political majority, be made the same for women as for men.

2d. That all laws relative to the inheritance and ownership of property, to the division and administration of estates, and to the execution of Wills, be made equally applicable to women and men.

3d. That mothers be entitled, equally with fathers, to become guardians of their children.

4th. That confirmed and habitual drunkenness, of either husband or wife, be held as sufficient ground for divorce; and that the temperate partner be appointed legal guardian of the children.

5th. That women be exempted from taxation until their right of suffrage is practically acknowledged.

6th. That women equally with men be entitled to claim trial before a jury of their peers.

These petitions should be firm and uncompromising in tone; and a hearing should be demanded before Committees specially empowered to consider and report them. In my judgment, the time is not distant, when such petitions will be granted, and when justice, the simple justice they ask, will be cordially, joyfully rendered.

I call then for the publication of a Declaration of Woman's Rights, accompanied by Forms of Petitions, by the National Woman's Rights Convention at their present session. In good hope,

Your friend and brother,   WILLIAM HENRY CHANNING.

Petition of Abby May Alcott and Others to the Citizens of Massachusetts on Equal Political Rights of Woman

(*Una*, November 1853)

Fellow-Citizens:—In May next a Convention will assemble to revise the Constitution of the Commonwealth.

At such a time it is the right and duty of every one to point out whatever he deems erroneous and imperfect in that instrument, and press its amendment on public attention.

We deem the extension to woman of all civil rights, a measure of vital importance to the welfare and progress of the State. On every principle of natural justice, as well as by the nature of our institutions, she is as fully entitled as man to vote, and to be eligible to office. In governments based on force, it might be pretended with some plausibility, that woman being supposed physically weaker than man, should be excluded from the State. But ours is a government professedly resting on the consent of the governed. Woman is surely as competent to give that consent as man. Our Revolution claimed that taxation and representation should be co-extensive. While the property and labor of women are subject to taxation, she is entitled to a voice in fixing the amount of taxes, and the use of them when collected, and is entitled to a voice in the laws that regulate punishments. It would be a disgrace to our schools and civil institutions, for any one to argue that a Massachusetts woman who has enjoyed the full advantage of all their culture, is not as competent to form an opinion on civil matters, as the illiterate foreigner landed but a few years before upon our shores—unable to read or write—by no means free from early prejudices, and little acquainted with our institutions. Yet such men are allowed to vote.

Woman as wife, mother, daughter, and owner of property, has important rights to be protected. The whole history of legislation so unequal between the sexes, shows that she can not safely trust these to the other sex. Neither have her rights as mother, wife, daughter, laborer, ever received full legislative protection. Besides, our institutions are not based on the idea of one class receiving protection from another; but on the well-recognized rule that each class, or sex, is entitled to such civil rights, as will enable it to protect itself. The exercise of civil rights is one of the best means of education. Interest in great questions, and the discussion of them under momentous responsibility, call forth all the faculties and nerve them to their fullest strength. The grant of these rights on the part of society, would quickly lead to the enjoyment by woman, of a share in the higher grades of professional employment. Indeed, without these, mere book study is often but a waste of time. The learning for which no use is found or anticipated, is too frequently forgotten, almost as soon as acquired. The influence of such a share, on the moral condition of society, is still more important. . . .

Some may think it too soon to expect any action from the Convention. Many facts lead us to think that public opinion is more advanced on this question than is generally supposed. Beside, there can be no time so proper to call public attention to a radical change in our civil polity as now, when the whole framework of our government is to be subjected to examination and discussion. It is never too early to begin the discussion of any desired change. To urge our claim on the Convention, is to bring our question before the proper tribunal, and secure at the same time the immediate attention of the general public. Massachusetts, though she has led the way in most other reforms, has in this fallen behind her rivals, consenting to learn, as to the protection of the property of married women, of many younger States. Let us redeem for her the old pre-eminence, and urge her to set a noble example in this the most important of all civil reforms. To this we ask you to join with us in the accompanying petition to the Constitutional Convention.

L. M. Alcott to Lucy Stone

Concord, Mass., Oct. 1, 1873

Dear Mrs. Stone:—I am so busy just now proving "Woman's Right to Labor" that I have no time to help prove "Woman's Right to Vote." When I read your note aloud to the family, asking "What shall I say to Mrs Stone?" my honored father instantly replied: "Tell her you are ready to follow your leader, sure that you could not have a better one." My brave old mother, with the ardor of many unquenchable Mays shining in her face, cried out: "Tell her I am seventy-three, but I mean to go to the polls before I die, even if my daughters have to carry me." And two little men already mustered in added the cheering words: "Go ahead, Aunt Weedy, we will let you vote as much as you like." Such being the temper of the small convention of which I am now President, I can not hesitate to say that though I may not be with you in the body I shall be in spirit, and I am, as ever, hopefully and heartily yours,

LOUISA MAY ALCOTT.

L. M. Alcott to Lucy Stone

Dear Mrs. Stone:—One should be especially inspired this Centennial year before venturing to speak or write. I am not so blest, and find myself so busy trying to get ready for the good time that is surely coming, I can only in a very humble way, help on the cause all women should have at heart.

As reports are in order, I should like to say a word for the girls, on whom in a great measure, depends the success of the next generation.

My lines fell in pleasant places last year, and I looked well about me as I went among the young people, who unconsciously gave me some very cheering facts in return for very poor fictions.

I was both surprised and delighted with the nerve and courage, the high aims and patient persistence which appeared, not only among the laborious young women whose teacher is necessity, but among tenderly nurtured girls who cherished the noblest ambitions and had learned to earn the happiness no wealth could buy them.

Having great faith in young America, it gave me infinite satisfaction to find such eager interest in all good things, and to see how irresistably the spirit of our new revolution, stirring in the hearts of sisters and daughters, was converting the fathers and brothers who loved them. One shrewd, business man said, when talking of Woman Suffrage, "How *can* I help believing in it, when I've got a wife and six girls who are *bound* to have it?"

And many a grateful brother declared he could not be mean enough to shut any door in the face of the sister who had made him what he was.

So I close this hasty note by proposing three cheers for the girls of 1876—and the hope that they will prove themselves worthy descendants of the mothers of this Revolution, remembering that

> "Earth's fanatics make
> Too often Heaven's saints."

Concord, June 29 [1876].   L. M. ALCOTT.

L. M. Alcott to The Woman's Journal

Editors Journal:—As other towns report their first experience of women at the polls, Concord should be heard from, especially as she has distinguished herself by an unusually well conducted and successful town meeting.

Twenty-eight women intended to vote, but owing to the omission of some formality several names could not be put upon the lists. Three or four were detained at home by family cares and did not neglect their domestic duties to rush to the polls as has been predicted. Twenty, however, were there, some few coming alone, but mostly with husbands, fathers or brothers as they should; all in good spirits and not in the least daunted by the awful deed about to be done.

Our town meetings I am told are always orderly and decent, this one certainly was; and we found it very like a lyceum lecture only rather more tedious than most, except when gentlemen disagreed and enlivened the scene with occasional lapses into bad temper or manners, which amused but did not dismay the women-folk, while it initiated them into the forms and courtesies of parliamentary debate.

Voting for school committee did not come till about three, and as the meeting began at one, we had ample time to learn how the mystic rite was performed, so, when at last our tickets were passed to us we were quite prepared to follow our leader without fear.

Mr. Alcott with a fatherly desire to make the new step as easy as possible for us, privately asked the moderator when the women were to vote, and on being told that they could take their chance with the men or come later, proposed that they should come first as a proper token of respect and for the credit of the town. One of the selectmen said "By all means;" and proved himself a tower of strength by seconding the philosopher on this momentous occasion.

The moderator (who is also the registrar and has most kindly and faithfully done his duty to the women in spite of his own difference of opinion) then announced that the ladies would prepare their votes and deposit them before the men did. No one objected, we were ready, and filed out in good order, dropping our votes and passing back to our seats as quickly and quietly as possible, while the assembled gentlemen watched us in solemn silence.

No bolt fell on our audacious heads, no earthquake shook the town, but a pleasing surprise created a general outbreak of laughter and applause, for, scarcely were we seated when Judge Hoar rose and proposed that the polls be closed. The motion was carried before the laugh subsided, and the polls were closed without a man's voting; a perfectly fair proceeding we thought since we were allowed no voice on any other question.

The superintendent of schools expressed a hope that the whole town would vote, but was gracefully informed that it made no difference as the women had all voted as the men would.

Not quite a correct statement by the way, as many men would probably have voted for other candidates, as tickets were prepared and some persons looked disturbed at being deprived of their rights. It was too late, however, for the joke became sober earnest, and the women elected the school committee for the coming year, feeling satisfied, with one or two exceptions, that they had secured persons whose past services proved their fitness for the office.

The business of the meeting went on, and the women remained to hear the discussion of ways and means, and see officers elected with neatness and dispatch by the few who appeared to run the town pretty much as they pleased.

At five the housewives retired to get tea for the exhausted gentlemen, some of whom certainly looked as if they would need refreshment of some sort after their labors. It was curious to observe as the women went out how the faces which had regarded them with disapproval, derision or doubt when they went in now smiled affably, while several men hoped the ladies would come again, asked how they liked it, and assured them that there had not been so orderly a meeting for years.

One of the pleasant sights to my eyes was a flock of school-boys watching with great interest their mothers, aunts and sisters, who were showing them how to vote when their own emancipation day came. Another was the spectacle of women sitting beside their husbands, who greatly enjoyed the affair though many of them differed in opinion and had their doubts about the Suffrage question.

Among the new voters were descendents of Major Buttrick of Concord fight renown, two of Hancock and Quincy, and others whose grandfathers or great grandfathers had been among the first settlers of the town. A goodly array of dignified and earnest women, though some of the "first families" of the historic town were conspicuous by their absence.

But the ice is broken, and I predict that next year our ranks will be fuller, for it is the first step that counts, and when the timid or indifferent, several of whom came to look on, see that we still live, they will venture to express publicly the opinions they held or have lately learned to respect and believe.

Concord, March 30, 1880.   L. M. A.

Editor Journal:—You ask what we are going to do about Municipal Suffrage for women in Concord? and I regret to be obliged to answer, as before—"Nothing but make a motion asking for it at town meeting, and see it promptly laid upon the table again."

It is always humiliating to have to confess this to outsiders, who look upon Concord as a representative town, and are amazed to learn that it takes no active part in any of the great reforms of the day, but seems to be content with the reflected glory of dead forefathers and imported geniuses, and falls far behind smaller but more wide awake towns with no pretensions to unusual intelligence, culture, or renown.

I know of few places where Municipal Suffrage might more safely be granted to our sex than this, for there is an unusually large proportion of tax-paying, well-to-do and intelligent women, who only need a little training, courage, and good leadership to take a helpful and proper share in town affairs. They would not ask or accept town offices, but would be glad to work in their own efficient and womanly way, as they have proved they could work by the success of their church, charity and social labors for years past.

To those who see what brave and noble parts women elsewhere are taking in the larger and more vital questions of the time, the thought very naturally comes: "What a pity that so much good sense, energy, time, and money could not be used for more pressing needs than church-fairs, tea-parties, or clubs for the study of pottery, Faust, and philosophy!"

While a bar room door stands open between two churches, and men drink themselves to death before our eyes, it seems as if Christian men and women should bestir themselves to try at least to stop it; else the commandment "Thou shalt love thy neighbor as thyself" is written over the altars in vain, and the daily prayer "Lead us not into temptation" is but empty breath.

If the women could vote on the license question I think the barroom would be closed; but while those who own the place say, "It would lessen the value of the property to make a temperance house of it," and the license matter is left to the decision of those men who always grant it, the women can only wait and hope and pray for the good time when souls are counted of more value than dollars, and law and gospel can go hand in hand.

A forty years acquaintance with the town leads me to believe that as the conservative elders pass away, the new generation will care less for the traditions of the past, more for the work of the present, and taking a brave part in it, will add fresh honors to the fine old town, which should be marching abreast with the foremost, not degenerating into a museum for revolutionary relics, or a happy hunting-ground for celebrity-seekers.

A rumor has just reached me that some of the husbands of our few Suffrage women intend to settle the license question in the right way, and perhaps say a good word for our petition before it is shelved. This is encouraging, for it shows that the power behind the throne is gently working, and though the good women have little to say in public, they do know how to plead, advise, and convince in private. So, even if fewer should vote this year than last, and if nothing seems to come of our effort to secure Municipal Suffrage this time, we shall not be disheartened, but keep stirring our bit of leaven, and wait, as housewives know how to do, for the fermentation which slowly but surely will take place, if our faith hope and charity are only strong, bright, and broad enough.

Concord, Mass., Feb. 4, 1882.   L. M. ALCOTT.

Concord, Mass., May 8, 1884.

Editors Woman's Journal:

There is very little to report about the woman's vote at Concord Town Meeting, as only eight were there in time to do the one thing permitted them.

With the want of forethought and promptness which show how much our sex have yet to learn in the way of business habits, some dozen delayed coming till the vote for school committee was over. It came third on the warrant, and a little care in discovering this fact would have spared us much disappointment. It probably made no difference in the choice of officers, as there is seldom any trouble about the matter, but it is to be regretted that the women do not give more attention to the duty which they really care for, yet fail, as yet, to realize the importance of, small as it is at present.

Their delay shows, however, that home affairs are *not* neglected, for the good ladies remained doubtless to give the men a comfortable dinner and set their houses in order before going to vote.

Next time I hope they will leave the dishes till they get home, as they do when in a hurry to go to the sewing-society, Bible-class, or picnic. A hasty meal once a year will not harm the digestion of the lords of creation, and the women need all the drill they can get in the new duties that are surely coming to widen their sphere, sharpen their wits, and strengthen their wills, teaching them the courage, intelligence and independence all should have, and many sorely need in a world of vicissitudes. A meeting should be called before the day for action comes, to talk over matters, to get posted as to time, qualification of persons, and the good of the schools; then the women can act together, know what they are doing, and keep up the proper interest all should feel in so important a matter.

"I come, but I'm lukewarm," said one lady, and that is the spirit of too many.

"We ought to have had a meeting, but you were not here to call it, so no one did," said another, as if it were not a very simple thing to open any parlor and ask the twenty-eight women voters to come and talk an hour.

It was a good lesson, and we hope there will be energy and foresight enough in Concord to register more names, have a quiet little caucus, and send a goodly number of earnest, wide-awake ladies to town-meeting next year.

LOUISA M. ALCOTT.

Louisa M. Alcott to the American Woman Suffrage Association

Concord [October 1885]

I should think it was hardly necessary for me to say that it is impossible for me ever to "go back" on woman suffrage. I earnestly desire to go forward on that line as far and as fast as the prejudices, selfishness and blindness of the world will let us, and it is a great cross to me that ill-health and home duties prevent my devoting heart, pen and time to this most vital question of the age. After a fifty years' acquaintance with the noble men and women of the anti-slavery cause and the sight of the glorious end to their faithful work, I should be a traitor to all I most love, honor and desire to imitate if I did not covet a place among those who are giving their lives to the emancipation of the white slaves of America.

If I can do no more, let my name stand among those who are willing to bear ridicule and reproach for the truth's sake, and so earn some right to rejoice when the victory is won.

Most heartily yours for woman suffrage and all other reforms.

Jo's Boys

(1886)

L. M. ALCOTT

[Nan to Jo's Boys]: "Let us have equal opportunities. . . . I like justice, and we get very little of it. . . . I went to a suffrage debate in the Legislature last winter; and of all the feeble, vulgar twaddle I ever heard, that was the worst; and those men were *our* representatives. . . . I want an intelligent man to represent *me,* if I can't do it myself, not a fool." . . .

"I have only one thing to say, and it is this, . . . I want to ask every boy of you what you really think on this subject. . . . Do you believe in Woman's Suffrage?" . . .

[A play performed at Plumfield:] *The Owlsdark Marbles* closed the entertainment, and, being something new, proved amusing to this very indulgent audience. The gods and goddesses on Parnassus were displayed in full conclave, and, thanks to Mrs. Amy's skill in draping and posing, the white wigs and cotton-flannel robes were classically correct and graceful, though sundry modern additions somewhat marred the effect, while adding point to the showman's learned remarks. Mr. Laurie was Professor Owlsdark in cap and gown; and, after a high-flown introduction, he proceeded to exhibit and explain his marbles. The first figure was a stately Minerva, but a second glance produced a laugh, for the words "Women's Rights" adorned her shield, a scroll bearing the motto "Vote early and often" hung from the beak of the owl perched on her lance, and a tiny pestle and mortar ornamented her helmet. Attention was drawn to the firm mouth, the piercing eye, the awe-inspiring brow, of the strong-minded woman of antiquity, and some scathing remarks made upon the degeneracy of her modern sisters who failed to do their duty.

Index